Akita

The Tears and Message of Mary

by
Teiji Yasuda, O.S.V.
English Version by John M. Haffert, 1989

101 Foundation, Inc.
Asbury, New Jersey 08802-0151
U.S.A.

TABLE OF CONTENTS:

✝✝✝

Akita—The Tears and Message of Mary

by Fr. Teiji Yasuda

Preface:

News of tears flowing from a statue of Our Lady in a convent in Akita, Japan, spread through the entire nation following a series of articles in the publication *Catholic Graph*. Over a considerable time newspapers, magazines, radio and television have covered these events.

Church authorities considered it prudent to remain quiet. It was only after twelve years of national publicity that Fr. Tatsuya Shimura, assistant rector of the Cathedral in Tokyo, decided courageously to publish a little work entitled *The Virgin Mary Weeps At Akita*. French and German translations of this little work caused news of the affair to spread in the west.

On Easter Sunday, 1984, 22nd of April, the Most Rev. John Ito, the Bishop directly responsible, issued a pastoral letter declaring "the events of Akita" to be supernatural. On November 3rd of the same year, the Bishop himself came to pray at the sanctuary of Yuzawadai (Akita) with a group of pilgrims. Since that time pilgrims have come in ever greater numbers from all parts of Japan and from other nations.

For thirteen years I was chaplain of the community of the Handmaids of the Eucharist in Akita and I related the "events of Akita" in our monthly bulletin during the last two years before writing this book.

It seemed to me opportune to gather the articles together in a complete work, which I hope will bring joy to those who have sustained us by their fervent prayer. I pray that it will justly and faithfully clarify the facts so that an ever greater number may progress in an understanding of the divine mysteries they reveal.

In the name of the community and all readers I thank Bishop Kei'ichi Sato, successor of Bishop Ito, who kindly approved the publication of this book without reserve. May it be for all, by the Grace of the Lord, an instrument of edification and of spiritual progress.

Given on the Feast of the Annunciation, March 25 1987, on the hill of Yuzawadai, Akita.

Signed,

Father Teiji Yasuda.

Prologue

As I write this, I have just spent almost thirteen years in the convent at Yuzawadai on the outskirts of Akita where I have been an eyewitness to the events I am about to describe.

A remarkable series of coincidences brought me to this holy place. The immediate occasion for my coming was an incident which took place because of sudden bad weather.

At the time I was stationed in Tokyo and had been invited to a city in the north to speak at a catechetical session. I took advantage of the occasion to go a little farther to my native village which I had not seen for sometime. It was in February of 1974. The weather was unstable and a snowstorm of exceptional violence paralyzed all communications for two days. I was held up at the village church with nothing in particular to do.

A member of the parish, seeing that I was free, asked if I would like to go to say Mass at the convent of the sisters of Yuzawadai. She explained that because of the heavy snowstorms during these past days, no one had been able to say Mass at the convent which was up along the hill on the outskirts of Akita.

Having no reason to refuse, I willingly agreed. Towards two o'clock that afternoon I took advantage of the offer of a neighbor who had a truck. The rough road which led to the convent had disappeared under a thick covering of snow. We finally made it with the help of a bulldozer which cleared the way. The little building, which I then saw for the first time, was quite poor. I cite here the note which I published in a parish bulletin a short time later:

"This winter I had the occasion to meet a group truly living the vow of poverty. About ten years ago a small group of women gathered together in a house on a hill outside Akita to lead a life of prayer. Some of them later left, others remained. They did not have a priest and lived on strict necessities, having abandoned all their goods in order to consecrate themselves to God.

"They seemed to be the butt of constant criticism and calumny. They were reproached for not having anything other to do, and if I listened to what was being said, perhaps

I might have been of the same opinion. One must not forget the truth contained in this paradox... the one who is despised becomes in reality the one who identifies most with Christ. This example suffices to teach us which one is more loved of God, the one who throws the insults or the one who receives them.

"These women told me of an unusual experience. They said: '*We were ardently begging the intercession of the Holy Virgin when there appeared on a hand of Her little statue, sculptured on a globe and leaning against a cross, a mark of red blood in the form of a cross. From this mark blood flowed. It remained more than three weeks accompanied by other phenomena expressing the sufferings of Mary.*'

"They then invited me to come and see the statue. I went to the chapel, said Mass there, and prayed to the Virgin Mary. I remained a moment to contemplate the statue of which the hand appeared to have bled. I felt very intensely that Mary had to suffer for the church of Japan, even to the point of shedding blood. I left the hill carrying in my heart a profound conviction that in this place there was an urgent appeal for prayer."

It was in these dispositions that I returned to my parish with a resolution to participate in some manner in the sufferings of Mary. A little later, I was led to give up my position as pastor and I at once remembered the Virgin who had shed blood. I felt an ardent desire to go there to pray.

Such were the circumstances which led me to the Virgin of Yuzawadai, and with the passage of time I cannot but recognize the hand of Divine Providence, watchful in everything.

Since I have been chaplain here in the Yuzawadai (Akita) convent, the statue of Mary has undergone several changes of appearance. It has been the subject of phenomena which natural laws cannot explain. The most remarkable of these are the tears which have flowed from both eyes, now known throughout Japan and the world.

I thank God for the grace for having been formed in prayer in this place where I hope to remain still a long time in order to make spiritual progress. I also pray that the numerous pilgrims who come in the future to pray to the Virgin of Akita will find courage and peace in this place of special grace.

On March 10th, 1974, I took up my place at the convent of Yuzawadai. The first work I undertook was the examination of the messages which Sister Agnes was said to have received from Mary and to study the mysterious events connected with the statue. I had to prepare a complete documentation.

I began by extracting passages from the intimate journal of Sr. Agnes which treated the events in such a way as to reveal the underlying factors. I had my report read to the religious of the community and submitted a copy to the Bishop of the diocese, Bishop Ito.

A little later, a journalist from the review *Catholic Graph* asked for an interview. I thought that would offer a good occasion to make the events public. The articles published by the *Catholic Graph* brought forth numerous reactions. Some were enthusiastic and some hostile, as one can easily imagine. In the first years following the events, there were violent protestations from certain parts and in particular from a part of the Catholic hierarchy which showed itself openly reticent.

Now that the tempest is over and the events have been recognized as supernatural by the Ordinary of the diocese, in my soul and in my conscience it appears to me the proper time to reveal these manifest signs of Divine Providence. That is the reason for this book.

The reader may be surprised at the long studies and the suffering which preceded the good news which took place in the month of May, 1984, when the events relative to the Virgin of Yuzawadai were finally recognized as supernatural by the Bishop in a pastoral letter addressed to all the members of the diocese. That declaration came only many years down a laborious road sowed with multiple complications.

In his pastoral letter, following repeated visits to Rome for consultation with the Sacred Congregation of the Doctrine of the Faith concerning the events of Yuzawadai, Bishop Ito, as Bishop of the Diocese, solemnly recognized their supernatural character after mature reflection and detailed examination. He certified that the message given by Our Lady of Akita contains no element which might cause harm to the faith of the people of God. As we look back down that laborious road of trial and examination, we marvel now at some of the fantastic objections which were raised, and even more fantastic "explanations" which were proposed to explain away the tears which flowed from the wooden statue, and the blood which flowed from its hand.

From the very beginning the theory of "ectoplasm" was in the forefront. This theory spread far and wide before the true facts were known and cast such doubt upon the entire matter that there was indifference to the important messages pronounced by Our Lady... messages which are the whole reason for these events of which we speak in this book.

In order to overcome this mountain of prejudice, a great deal of patience and confidence in Divine Providence was necessary. It was *only after ten years* that the thesis of ectoplasm was officially rejected by competent ecclesiastical authority.

The theory, according to which the phenomena had a diabolical origin, was rejected by the facts themselves. As the proverb says: "One recognizes the truth by its fruits," and how many graces have been obtained by persons who came to honor the Virgin Mary in this place where She so signally manifested Her presence and delivered a message of major importance for the world! How many found the faith again, or were confirmed in the faith, and how many were cured of an incurable malady! There are many examples.

In his pastoral letter, the Bishop cites the special case of Teresa Chun, a Korean woman who was reduced to a vegetable state as a result of a brain tumor. She was cured miraculously during an apparition of the Virgin of Akita. Another confirming cure is that of the deafness of Sister Agnes who had been declared incurable. Our Lady Herself had announced this cure which took place in a single instant.

All the reasons above contributed to the official declaration by Bishop Ito which has opened the way to authentic veneration of the Virgin of Akita.

May the Lord be blessed for so many benefits and may our joy and gratitude ever increase!

TRANSLATOR'S NOTE:

From Father Yasuda's prologue, we learn that this is a book *written by an eyewitness.* Events attributed to Divine Providence brought this eyewitness, a sincere priest, to the Yuzawadai convent in Akita. Most of what you are about to read was compiled from his "news bulletins."

We also learn that an ecclesiastical commission found the events to be supernatural despite a theory of "ectoplasm" which for some years was the basis of great opposition, even from members of the Japanese hierarchy. By the time the Bishop of Niigata issued his pastoral letter of approval in 1984, the all-important message was obscured by the disputed signs which accompanied it... signs which had been given by God (as the pastoral states) to confirm the message.

Distracting Events

Also at Fatima, there were many extraordinary signs and a still undisclosed secret which have tended to distract us from the message. If we ask someone, "Do you know about Our Lady of Fatima?" how often the answer is, "Oh, yes! Isn't there some kind of secret?" or, "Wasn't there some kind of miracle?" Rarely do we meet persons who *know the message* to which Our Lady of Fatima attached a promise to avoid atomic war and bring "an era of peace to mankind!"

Some of the extraordinary signs Father Yasuda is about to describe in the following pages recall some of the "signs" seen at Fatima: *A globe of light* was seen coming from the East and resting above the tree upon which Our Lady appeared to the children; *the tree itself*, on one occasion, bent down under an unseen weight; inexplicable *sounds* were heard; what appeared to be flower petals fell *like snow* over the area; finally, at the time and place predicted by Our Lady, a great fire appeared in the sky *like the sun* whirling on itself, then plunged toward the earth. Suddenly the entire area, which had been soaked by a heavy rain, was *completely dry.*

First Person Account

One of the special aspects of this book by Father Yasuda is that he himself was *actually involved.* Our Lady Herself was to reveal that *She had chosen Fr. Yasuda for this task.* This gives remarkable credibility to all that Fr. Yasuda says and fortunately he not only reports the events, but he frequently interrupts to explain them.

7.

When Bishop Ito asked me to translate this book, I was reluctant to do so. I asked the Bishop if I might not rather write a book based on Fr. Yasuda's book and also on other works, such as that of Father Shimura, but the Bishop replied firmly that before anything else, *this* book should be made available in its full, original form.

I soon came to realize the wisdom and importance of this mandate. I recalled that in 1972, the centenary of the apparitions of Our Lady of Pontmain, the Rector of the Shrine of Pontmain gave me the privilege of translating the original account of the apparitions written by a priest within two days of their happening. It was the classic, most authentic and detailed account of the Pontmain apparitions.

It is an even greater privilege to have been given a mandate from Bishop Ito to translate Fr. Yasuda's book, which is not only the classic and most authentic account of what happened in Akita, but it will probably be to Akita what the memoirs of Sister Lucia are to Fatima.

J. M. H.

✝✝✝

Above: John Haffert, with hand on the shoulder of Sr. Agnes, standing in front of their convent with the Akita Community.

Chapter One

Vessel of Suffering

Born prematurely, Sister Agnes Katsuko Sasagawa (called Sister Agnes in the rest of our text) always had a weak constitution, but thanks to the love with which she was surrounded by her family, her personality developed under the best conditions.

She suffered her first great trial at the age of 19 when she was struck by a paralysis of the central nervous system following a mistake during an appendectomy. She became immobilized for 16 years, during which she was transferred from hospital to hospital undergoing one operation after the other.

In a clinic in Myoko she developed a friendship with a nurse who was a fervent Catholic. Thanks to the devoted care of this nurse, the state of the sick girl improved and it was here that she took her first steps in the Christian faith.

Her heart now awakened to the love of God, she soon felt within herself an ardent desire to become devoted to the service of God and of her neighbor. She wanted to enter a religious community but her family feared because of her health. After overcoming the reticence of her family, she was admitted to the community of the Sisters of Junshin in Nagasaki. However four months later she had a relapse and had to be taken back to the clinic of Myoko.

This time she spent ten days in a coma and her condition became critical. She was given some Lourdes water to drink which had been sent by the sisters of Nagasaki. Hardly had the water entered her mouth than she regained consciousness and her frozen limbs regained their mobility.

She decided to return to the convent of Our Lady of Junshin after a period of recovery, but the pastor of Takada persuaded her to take care of a newly constructed church in Myoko. Later, she heard about the Institute of the Handmaids of the Eucharist, a community in which one could live a consecrated life while remaining in society. Upon the invitation of Bishop Ito, founder of the Institute, she joined the Handmaids, retaining care of the church of Myoko which was near the hospital. In addition to caring for the church she taught catechism.

Such, in brief, is the road traveled by Sister Agnes up to the time of her first contact with the community of the Handmaids of the Eucharist.

In the first part of her life, with its numerous trials, one can already clearly discern the providential action of God. But since we are concerned especially about the life of Sister Agnes after she entered the community of the Handmaids, we will not return to the past, except as it may bear upon the important matters we have to relate.

New Trial

After 16 years of physical suffering and repeated hospitalization, who would expect a new and completely different affliction? But towards the end of January of 1973, Sister Agnes began to notice a diminution of hearing in both ears, but she was too taken up by the work of the church to pay much attention to it. However, on Friday, the 16th of March, when she went to answer a telephone call from the Motherhouse of the Handmaids, she suddenly realized that she had completely lost her hearing. She heard the bell, but when she took up the telephone she found herself plunged into total silence. The pastor found her sitting in the church stupefied by what had just happened to her. He took her at once to the hospital of Niigata.

Doctor Sawada, an Ear, Nose and Throat Specialist, had already cared for her in another hospital some years before due to a lack of hearing in her left ear. This time, a detailed examination revealed complete deafness of the right ear. *The diagnosis was one of evolving and incurable deafness!*

Sister Agnes at this time was in a state of extreme fatigue. She was immediately hospitalized to follow a treatment and rest cure. Afterwards, she took an intensive course in lip reading in order to regain social contact. She continued with uninterrupted training during the succeeding 43 days until she left the hospital. In her intimate journal, she notes the warnings and counsels of Doctor Sawada:

"It is very difficult to live in a world without sound. You are fortunate to have faith. I think that will help you. Do not become discouraged. We will take care of all the neccessary formalities in order that upon leaving the hospital you will be able to receive support for the physically handicapped. We will do everything possible to facilitate your social reintegration..."

She tells with gratitude of the attention and the encouragement of numerous persons during her hospitalization. She was sustained in her efforts to learn lip reading by the devoted personnel and also by the precious cooperation of relatives and close friends. Rather than hastening to say what they wanted to tell her, they took pains to articulate slowly, thus accelerating her progress. She was visited by some 300 friends who had known her at the church of Myoko. These visits buoyed her up like rays of sunshine, so necessary in the struggle against depression.

During her stay in the hospital she thought very much, as is quite natural, about what she would do as a deaf person. If she could no longer teach catechism, her family would surely want her to come back to them. But she had chosen to become consecrated to God and desired above all to live only in His service. Might it be permitted to her to offer herself in a life of prayer and penance in the Motherhouse of the Handmaids of the Eucharist? This was her most ardent desire.

And now, may I interrupt for a moment to make a personal remark? It was on Friday, the 16th of March, 1973, when Sister Agnes was suddenly and brusquely plunged into a world of total silence, and there is a coincidence in this which is a sign of Divine Providence.

The 16th of March, which marked the beginning of this deafness (which would be miraculously cured on May 30, 1982, following a promise of the Virgin in Her first message), is the vigil of the day when the Catholic Church of Japan commemorates the discovery in 1865 of the descendants of the "hidden Christians" on the site of O'ura in Nagasaki. To the French missionary who arrived there shortly after the reopening of the country, these "hidden Christians" made themselves known by asking, "*Where is the statue of the Virgin?"* This is a celebrated fact in the annals of the Church in Japan.

Thus the Lord began by submerging His instrument into total silence with the intention of communicating to the world the message of which we shall soon be speaking. Does not her silence recall the silence of the Japanese Christians of the feudal period? The hidden mission of Sister Agnes began this day, and *the cure of her deafness would become a sign of the authenticity of a heavenly message for the Church of Japan and for the world.*

Does not the Bible offer us analogous examples? The mission of Saint John the Baptist, "a voice which cries in the wilderness," was prepared by the trial of his father Zachary who had to remain deaf and dumb for a determined time. It is sometimes by means upsetting to man that the All Powerful deploys the force of His arm to reveal His unfathomable designs.

The Hill of Hope

Because of her handicap, Sister Agnes' family most definitely wanted her to return home. She showed herself so resolute, however, that her parents and her brother finally gave in. She received a letter from the Handmaids of the Eucharist who proposed that she come to dwell on the Hill of Yuzawadai, on the outskirts of Akita. This was also the counsel given by Bishop Ito. Since this was her own most ardent desire, she felt growing in her a new hope!

To her great astonishment, the only one who continued to oppose this decision was the beloved nurse who had become her Godmother and who had led to her conversion to Catholicism. The nurse argued that she should return to the hospital for a complete recovery.

This attitude of a person so dear saddened Sister Agnes. But even the beloved nurse finally gave in before the arguments of her elder brother and her sister-in-law who had shared her affection and were able to convince her diplomatically. Now the way was finally free!

On May 12th, 1973, leaving her home, Sister Agnes arrived at the convent in Yuzawadai accompanied by her sister and her sister-in-law. Welcomed like a member of the family by the six religious of the community, Sister Agnes thanked the Lord for the joy and the consolation brought to her by the prospect of a new life... a life in total silence, but a life in total prayer and dedication.

However, once she had left home, skepticism rose again among her relatives who could not decide to send her luggage, thinking, from one moment to the other that she would perhaps return. Sister Agnes experienced a similar hesitation, asking her spiritual director if she might not be overestimating herself. The chaplain, who at that time had been directing the little community for five years, was very understanding. He assured her that her mission was indeed to remain on the Hill with the Handmaids.

Finally, her affairs had been put in order. After ten days of waiting she was installed in her cell, and at that moment she was filled with a great peace. It was as though she had lived there always.

Unfortunately the chaplain who had encouraged her left a short time after her arrival. Sister Agnes was all the more saddened by this because daily Mass was no longer assured.

A Mysterious Light

The first of the "extraordinary events of Akita" took place on June 12th, 1973, when Sister Agnes was left to watch the house while the other members of the community went to Niigata to take part in a meeting of catechists. The superior had given her permission to open the door of the tabernacle for a time of adoration.

On this day, when she was in the chapel, an unusual phenomenon occurred. *A brilliant light* suddenly appeared as though *coming from the tabernacle.*

In her intimate journal, Sister Agnes describes in detail this astonishing experience as was requested of her by Bishop Ito: "When I approached to open the door of the tabernacle, as the superiors indicated, an overwhelming unknown light suddenly shone forth. Seized with emotion I prostrated myself immediately with my face to the floor.

"Evidently I no longer felt the audacity to open the tabernacle. I remained perhaps an hour in this position.

Subjugated by a power which overwhelmed me, I remained immobile, incapable of raising my head, even after the light had disappeared. When I came back to myself and I was finally able to reflect on what had happened, I asked myself if Jesus, present in the Host, had manifested Himself to enlighten my soul in the state of sin or if I had been simply a victim of hallucination.

"I had often opened the door of the tabernacle for adoration during the time that I was a catechist in the church in Myoko, but never had any such thing happened so it was all the more disquieting for me. Had I perhaps become crazy? I returned to pray in the chapel, but this time nothing happened. Whatever the case, it was an experience so unexpected that I went to bed that night without breathing a word about it to anyone."

The following morning Sister Agnes took advantage of an early awakening to go to the chapel an hour before the others. She was anxious to know if the light of the previous day had been nothing but an illusion of a moment. When with joined hands she approached the back of the altar where the tabernacle was, she was again struck by the blinding light. She recoiled instinctively and prostrated herself in adoration. Truly, it was neither an illusion nor a dream. Jesus, present in the Host, had truly manifested Himself. *Now she was sure.* After the light disappeared, she remained prostrate. Soon the other sisters arrived for Lauds, but she was still under the effect of this force which overwhelmed her as she mechanically recited the common prayers.

The following Thursday, the 14th of June, while she was praying before the Blessed Sacrament with her companions, Sister Agnes again saw the light flash forth, but this time it was surrounded by a red flame which seemed to envelop the rays shining from the tabernacle. The extremity of the flame was golden. All the tabernacle appeared in flames. She was overcome and immediately prostrated herself.

In her journal, she describes the state of prostration which increased in the course of these three extraordinary days: "I could not think of anything but to adore and to render thanks before the Blessed Sacrament. When I left the chapel and regained my normal state, I no longer felt that interior sweetness which I cannot find words to explain. Doubts assailed me. Had I lost my head?

"After some time, it occurred to me that if this was not a mental apparition, perhaps others had seen the same thing. With a lively desire of knowing, I slipped in some words about the unknown light during breakfast. Indeed, no one seemed to be aware of it and I quickly closed my lips without saying more. The superior remarked, 'You are without doubt the only one concerned, so don't speak of it.' Taken up short, I simply acquiesced with a nod of the head."

This third experience, which took place between 8 and 9:30 in the morning, seems to have left the strongest impression and the most indelible memory upon Sister Agnes. Her steps led her spontaneously towards the chapel and her heart overflowed with praises for Jesus present in the Eucharist. Memory of the mysterious phenomenon revived in her a sentiment of inexpressible happiness, a plenitude of joy which inflamed her heart with love for God. She herself explains in these simple words:

"At the moment when I write these lines, it is the same joy which seized me, an ardent desire for the Lord which invaded all my being."

Meditation

Again, I would like to interrupt to remark that one can say the vision of celestial light appeared like an invitation addressed to Sister Agnes in particular (as following events will confirm). Saint Paul, on the road to Damascus, owed his conversion and his mission to the meeting of a brilliant light coming from heaven. When he heard the Voice say to him, "Why persecuteth thou me?" he fell prostrate with his face against the ground while his companions were standing about him. This was because Paul must have been the only one to see the influence of the celestial light.

The companions of Sister Agnes, who shared the same roof and performed the same spiritual exercises, received absolutely nothing. This was the first invitation to a particular mission which began then and which was addressed specifically to her. At Fatima, the three shepherds were first of all struck with amazement at the sight of a brilliant light. It was the sign of the approaching visit of the Virgin. Likewise, the light which overwhelmed Sister Agnes seems like a preparation for the great message which was about to be confided to her by the Mother of God.

The mysterious light from the Blessed Sacrament reveals the very nature of Jesus who says, "*I am the Light of the world.*"

As we shall learn later, the miraculous cure of the deafness of Sister Agnes (promised by Our Lady as a sign of the authenticity of the events) took place during Benediction of the Blessed Sacrament. Thus the meeting with the light also takes on, for Sister Agnes, a prophetic value.

TRANSLATOR'S NOTE:

The light at Fatima which preceded the Apparition of Our Lady, so distracted the children that they were still wondering about the brilliance of the light when they noted Our Lady in its midst. She asked if they would be willing to accept whatever God would send them and offer it up for the conversion of sinners and in reparation for sin. When the children replied that they would, Our Lady opened Her hands and *rays of that intense light suddenly streamed from Her heart* causing the children to feel "Lost in God," and to exclaim, "Oh, most Holy Trinity, I adore Thee, My God, My God, I love Thee *in the Most Blessed Sacrament!*"

When Bishop Ito was asked "What is the message of Our Lady Of Akita," he answered simply, "It is the message of Our Lady of Fatima." And there is a remarkable similarity between the light of the Eucharist seen at Fatima, shining from the Immaculate Heart of Mary and the light from the tabernacle announcing to Sister Agnes (in a way she could not yet fully understand) that as Our Lady had revealed a most important message at Fatima, so now that message was to be reaffirmed at Akita through this humble Handmaid of the Eucharist.

†††

Chapter Two

Angels In The Light

After those three days when an extraordinary light shone forth from the tabernacle, an entire week passed without anything out of the ordinary happening. On the afternoon of June 23rd, the Bishop arrived at the convent. The following day, Sunday, was the Feast of Corpus Christi.

This feast would be most important to the Handmaids of the Eucharist at any time. However, with the arrival of the Bishop, they rejoiced particularly that day because they had been without a chaplain since the 5th of June, having to go almost three weeks without daily Mass, and also without news of another chaplain coming.

The Bishop celebrated the Mass of the Blessed Sacrament and, as founder of the community, he gave them these words of encouragement: "This community, consecrated to the Blessed Sacrament, should practice in a special way devotion to the Heart of Christ present in the Eucharist."

His Excellency remained a week on the Hill giving guidance and counsel.

During the three days following the Feast of the Blessed Sacrament, adoration (from 8 until 9 in the morning) was made by four sisters. One was Sister Agnes. After hymns, Rosary, and common prayers, there followed silent meditation. The number of sisters present was so small that the words of Christ seemed to be for them: "When two or more are gathered in my name, there am I in the midst of them." The sisters were united in praise. The heart of Sister Agnes was absorbed in a special way in the Eucharistic adoration. She writes in her journal:

"During these three days of retreat, I felt myself burning with love for the Lord, filled with the desire to consecrate myself entirely to Him."

Thursday was the eve of the Feast of the Sacred Heart. Since the change in the calendar, this Feast no longer had its previous solemnity but continued to have a special honor for the Handmaids of the Eucharist. During adoration after the morning Mass, the program was the same as the preceding days. To better understand what happened shortly after the beginning of the silent meditation, we turn again to Sister's journal (with the addition of clarifying details which she furnished later):

"Suddenly, the blinding light shone from the Blessed Sacrament. As previously, something like fog or smoke began to gather around the altar and the rays of light. *Then there appeared a multitude of beings similar to angels who surrounded the altar in adoration before the Host.*"

The word "angel" did not at once occur to Sister Agnes. As we will see later, she was embarrassed when she tried to explain to the Bishop what she had seen in the light. She said, "These were not human beings, but one could see very clearly that they were an adoring crowd of spiritual beings." When the Bishop remarked that they must have been angels, then she began to use this word. Furthermore, she used the word "multitude" because it seemed to her that from the moment of their appearance, the space around seemed to open up into a sort of infinite depth. She continues:

"Absorbed by this surprising spectacle, I knelt down to adore. Then I was seized with the thought that there could be a fire outside. Turning around to look through the bay window in the back, I saw that there was no fire outside. It was indeed the altar which was enveloped in this mysterious light. The brightness from the Host was so brilliant that I could not look at It directly. Closing my eyes, instinctively I prostrated myself. When the hour of adoration was over I remained in the same position without noticing that the others had left."

Then the superiors came and tapped her on the shoulder to ask that she watch the house during their absence. All disappeared. Suddenly the chapel looked as it always had before.

As she was in care of the house, and since it was not yet time to prepare for lunch, she went upstairs to the sewing room to continue her work but her thoughts remained so absorbed in what she had just seen that she had difficulty managing the needle.

The Bishop's Guidance

The Bishop was remaining there for the entire week to give the sisters conferences and say daily Mass for them. About 3 o'clock in the afternoon of that same day Sister Agnes carried tea to the Bishop. As she went to his room she said to herself:

"Should I not confide these things to the Bishop in order that he might counsel me in truth? If I keep it to myself might I not lose my mind? May it not be even now that I am suffering hallucinations? And if truly I have hallucinations and fall sick, what trouble for my companions! Now is the time to be courageous and to tell everything to the Bishop. He will know indeed how to enlighten and guide me."

Having taken this decision, and despite the difficulty she had in doing so, she began her recital to him. The Bishop listened with serious attention which encouraged her so much that she felt free to pour out her soul to him frankly, telling all that happened. When finally she had finished, she felt consoled, as if someone had lifted a great weight from her shoulders.

The Bishop gave her the following counsel: "As it would be impossible at the moment to know exactly the nature of the phenomena you have seen, you should not speak to anyone about them and be careful not to think only of these things. Above all, you must be careful not to say to yourself 'only I saw this because I am a special case' or to have similar proud thoughts. You must force yourself to progress in humility and continue to lead the normal everyday life with the others without changing anything. What you have told me does not seem to me to come from any derangement of mind and you have nothing to fear on that score. Such phenomena can happen.

"You know that the Virgin also appeared to the shepherds at Fatima... In your case, we do not know exactly what this may be. So keep silent and continue your life without changing anything. Meditate and pray before the Blessed Sacrament."

Sister Agnes left comforted and reassured by this wise counsel.

Apparition of the Angel

The next day, Friday, June 29th, was the Feast of the Sacred Heart. The Bishop preached on devotion to the Eucharist. Of course Sister Agnes, unable to hear anything, had to follow the homily by reading the Bishop's lips. Nevertheless, her heart was seized with love for the Sacred Heart of Jesus and was lost in fervent prayer throughout the entire service.

Sister Agnes and the superioress were assigned to the Hour of Adoration from 9 to 10 in the morning. Sister Agnes went to the Chapel a half hour early to pray silently before the Blessed Sacrament. Soon the superioress arrived and they knelt together before the tabernacle. Reading on the lips of her companion that she was inviting her to begin the Rosary, Sister Agnes took her beads and they began with the usual opening hymn in honor of the Eucharist. They were about to begin the Rosary when a mysterious phenomenon occurred.

"At the instant when I took my Rosary to begin, a person appeared very close to me on my right," Sister Agnes relates in her journal. She wrote:

"Before I continue, I should explain something which happened four years before. I was a catechist in Myoko and I had fainted because of a high fever caused by a virus infection. I had to be taken to the hospital and it seems that I was four days in a coma, completely cut off from the exterior world. The thermometer indicated a very high temperature. On the evening of the second day when a priest gave me the Sacrament of the Sick, I very clearly recited the Our Father, the Hail Mary, the Gloria and the Apostles Creed in Latin, without knowing that I did it. Immediately afterwards, I did not know how to answer the priest who asked me where I had learned Latin. Indeed, I had never learned it to the point of knowing these prayers by heart any more than I would be able to say them now. If there had not been witnesses there, I would not have believed it.

"My mother recounts that all the time I was praying, my face seemed in a light and my hands were crossed on my breast. As for me, I remember that I saw a beautiful person in a place which seemed like a pleasant field. This person with a movement of the hand, had invited me to approach her. But I was hindered from doing it by people as thin as living skeletons who gripped at me. Looking beyond, I saw a crowd of persons who were fighting each other to reach a level of pure water, but one after the other they fell into a river of dirty water. Filled with compassion for these poor people, I prayed also for them. I said especially the mysteries of the Rosary. Then I suddenly saw on the right side of my bed a gracious person whom I did not know and who began to pray the Rosary with me. After the first decade she added a prayer I did not know. Surprised, I repeated it after her. Then she counseled me to add this after each decade. The words are:

"'Oh my Jesus, forgive us our sins, save us from the fires of hell, lead all souls to heaven and especially those who are most in need of your mercy.'

"A friend who was watching at my bedside at that very moment was about to leave on the advice of my mother, because it was getting very late, but she remained a little longer in order to hear this unknown prayer to the end. As for myself, the words of the prayer remained engraved in my memory and I never fail to add them after each decade.

"A short time afterwards, a Salesian priest asked me to teach it to him and wanted to know where I had learned it. Later, I received a letter from him saying that this prayer had been taught by the Virgin to the children at Fatima, that there had not yet been a definitive translation into Japanese, but it was indeed in this manner that the prayer should be said. It is thus that I came to know the precious origin of this prayer."

(Let us remember that Sister Agnes was kneeling with the superioress in Adoration on the Feast of the Sacred Heart and in her journal she was about to tell us that suddenly a person had appeared on her right side as she was about to begin to say the Rosary with her companion. She interrupted to tell us of the above, and now she continues:)

"My going back has been a little long, but I did so to explain that the person who suddenly appeared on my right in the Chapel of the Convent on the Feast of the Sacred

Heart was *none other than the very person who appeared at my side in the hospital.* Gathering my strength, I squeezed the beads of the Rosary while slowly saying the prayers as the heavenly person did also. Believing myself dreaming although awake, I no longer paid attention to the sister beside me, even though I was fully aware of her. After the invocation, 'Our Lady of the Most Holy Rosary pray for us,' the heavenly person disappeared.

"Following was the time of silent prayer. Suddenly, I saw the blinding light. I immediately prostrated myself in adoration and when I lifted my eyes, I saw a soft light which enveloped the altar like a mist or a dense smoke in which appeared a cohort of angels turned towards the Blessed Sacrament whose pure and clear voices proclaimed 'Holy, Holy, Holy.' When they finished I heard a voice on my right praying:

"'Most Sacred Heart of Jesus, (TRULY) present in the Holy Eucharist, I consecrate my body and soul to be entirely one with Your Heart, being sacrificed at every instant on all the altars of the world and giving praise to the Father, pleading for the coming of His Kingdom.

"'Please receive this humble offering of myself. Use me as You will for the glory of the Father and the salvation of souls.

"'Most Holy Mother of God, never let me be separated from Your Divine Son. Please defend and protect me as Your special child. Amen.'"

TRANSLATOR'S NOTE:

Not spoken here, the word TRULY was added later by Our Lady and this prayer is an important part of the Message of Akita. It was composed by Bishop Ito for his community. The prayer asks Jesus to use us, body and soul, as one with His Sacred Heart, in order that we may be a part of His Sacrifice, part of His Adoration, part of His Love.

Finally we pray to Our Lady that She may help us in this union with the Sacred Heart of Her Son through the purity and light of Her own Immaculate Heart so that we will never be separated from Her Divine Son, and She will look upon us as "belonging" to Her as a very special and real child.

This prayer is essentially similar to the Morning Offering of the World Apostolate of Fatima (*The Blue Army*).

Sister Agnes continues: "This was the prayer of the Handmaids of the Eucharist which I knew well and which I recited aloud. During this prayer, I heard the voice of the same heavenly person who had come to my side in the hospital in Myoko. It seemed even more beautiful and pure when she recited these prayers than when she had told me in the hospital, 'Add these words after each decade.' The sound of her voice resounded in my ears like a true echo of heaven. With all my heart, I prayed with her when suddenly, there appeared a sort of symbol on the back of the Bishop who seemed to be kneeling in front of me. Also, I had a fleeting vision of seven or eight members of our Institute on both sides of the Bishop holding the red cord of his tunic.

"These visions disappeared when the prayer was over. I do not remember how long I remained still kneeling in prayer when the superioress came to tap me on the shoulder. Coming back to myself, I finished the adoration singing the *Ave* of Lourdes with her.

"Now, since the Bishop had asked me to report to him any extraordinary event, I went to tell him what I had just seen. "When I asked him if he had a symbol on his habit, he answered that he did not. When I spoke of the Chalice and the Host over an 'M' he was surprised and exclaimed, 'That is my episcopal insignia!'

"When I told him about the seven or eight members of the Institute holding the red cord of his tunic he seemed thoughtful."

The superioress who had been praying beside Sister Agnes on that morning of the Feast of the Sacred Heart said she was surprised when they began the Rosary and Sister Agnes recited it so slowly. "When I asked her why, she said that she was following the tempo of the angel."

But only Sister Agnes saw the light which again leapt forth from the Blessed Sacrament, this time with angels coming forth from the depth of the light.

What is the meaning of this Vision?

When one speaks of angels in adoration, one's imagination may conjure up vaporous scenes. Indeed, concerning the angels there is very little that is known from the theological point of view. In the Bible it is not rare to find accounts of spiritual beings around the throne of God singing without ceasing "Holy, Holy, Holy," and also incidents of men communicating with angels. In the present case, it appeared that these events were to prepare Sister Agnes for the messages of Our Lady, about which we are soon to hear.

Sister Agnes says that a very beautiful person appeared to her while she was in the hospital in Myoko. This person recited the Rosary with her and taught her the prayer which the Virgin Herself had given to the shepherds at Fatima. And who would be capable of such a prodigy if not an angel?

As I said in the beginning, it was only shortly after this that I arrived at the Convent through a set of unexpected circumstances and I therefore was able to know Sister Agnes and to counsel her. And in the course of the nine years that I have known her, this person appeared to her many times, guiding her, advising her, sometimes even reprimanding. And she assured me over and over that this person was not just an image, but a beautiful and very real being who appeared especially during prayer. And it is clear that this person's teachings and counsels in no way translated the subjective desires or wishes of the Sister. Sifting through my long experience as a priest, I believe that these numerous interventions and the advice received could come only from an angel.

As I said before, Sister Agnes did not use this word in the beginning. But after speaking to the Bishop who remarked that it must have been an angel she began to use the term. And finally, in the course of time, the angel, *appearing to Sister Agnes in the form of a woman, identified herself as her guardian angel.*

If I dwell on this, it is because these first visits of the angel are crucial to understanding the profound meaning of the events which follow, through which Our Lady wished to give the world a most important message.

We should not be surprised by the intervention of Sister Agnes' guardian angel. Saint Catherine Laboure was led to the chapel of the Rue du Bac during the night of July 18, 1830. "Come to the chapel," the angel said. "The Holy Virgin is waiting for you."

At Akita, as at Fatima, some parts of the message were conveyed by the angel. Yet in the case of Fatima, some say the approval of the apparitions there was somewhat delayed because of the role of the angels, but now, in retrospect, we see that the apparitions of the angels are an integral and most important aspect of the Fatima revelations. It was the angels who spoke to the children of the True Presence of Jesus in the Eucharist "Body, Blood, Soul and Divinity."

It is helpful to follow the chronological order of the events; all of which, of course, help us to understand the great message which God wishes by this means to give to the world at this moment.

Chapter Three

A Wound in the Hand

The day following the Feast of the Sacred Heart, which is now the Feast of the Immaculate Heart of Mary, the Bishop finished his stay of one week and was about to return to Niigata. He called Sister Agnes to his room and told her that she could prepare to take her vows. Not able to believe her good fortune, she asked for confirmation. She indeed received the same answer she had read on the Bishop's lips.

"I was so happy to receive this authorization that I would have cried out with joy. For me, it was an unspeakable joy to be able to consecrate myself entirely to God in this official way. My emotion was such that I could hardly find the words to thank him."

But since Thursday evening, another mysterious event had occurred. While praying in the chapel, Sister Agnes felt as though something pierced the palm of her hand. She was concerned because she had never before experienced such a pain. The following morning this was prolonged during the Mass and redoubled in intensity during the adoration.

When she left the chapel, she furtively spread her fingers which she had held closed tight. There in the center of her palm were two red scratches in the form of a cross. "What was that?" she asked herself. She was deeply concerned, thinking it was perhaps a sign of the measure of her sinfulness.

The wound was two centimeters wide and three centimeters long and appeared very large in the center of her hand. The pain was intense and the aspect of the wound was very different from what one is accustomed to see. This does not seem to have been caused with a blade. Even if she had held a small cross in her hand there would have remained a light cross pressed into the skin. It was as though a cross had been *engraved* in the skin. Of a color bordering on rose, it was not repulsive as other wounds and it seemed to give off even a certain beauty. Now, on Saturday (which would be the Feast of the Immaculate Heart), the pain persisted, but it didn't seem to get worse. Sister Agnes bore it in silence despite the pain she experienced. Since the way she kept her hand closed drew the attention of the superioress, Sister Agnes timidly showed her her hand.

"What in the world could that mean?"

"It is truly because of my sins!"

Examining it more closely, the superioress, amazed, could not help exclaiming, "What a strange color!" Then she chided her, "Why did you not show it to the Bishop before he left?" Sister Agnes could find no other response than, "I was afraid."

Indeed, why did she not show it to the Bishop? Sister Agnes was asking herself the same question. "I was afraid," is how she described her instinctive reaction. And in her dialect, the word she used to express this fear is a word which means fear mixed with respect, rather than just plain "fear" as we usually understand the word. She was filled with feelings of respect and fear which seemed to impose silence upon her, because she was confronted with a phenomenon which she could only attribute to a supernatural force. Further, it was so different from the preceding events that she esteemed it of secondary importance *because she alone was concerned.* The fact is that she hesitated to make anything of it before others. Furthermore, she had suffered illnesses and trials from her youth. She was accustomed to bearing suffering without making anything of it... and it seemed best, as she later justified, to be silent.

On the following Thursday, the 5th of July, while Sister Agnes was in adoration between 8:30 and 10 o'clock, the angel came again and recited the Rosary with her. With the angel, the praise became more authentic, more fervent.

In the evening, towards the middle of the 6 o'clock prayer, her left hand suddenly was pierced with a sharp pain. It was as though someone had thrust a pick into her palm. It was all she could do to keep herself from crying out. But the prayer was more important; with difficulty she succeeded in continuing to the end.

When she found herself alone again in the chapel, Sister Agnes wanted to look at the wound, but the pain was so great that she could not open her hand. Once she had left the chapel, she finally succeeded in opening her hand. At the center of the two branches of the cross there was now a hole from which blood flowed.

The evening meal was ready, but she had no desire to eat. However, not to draw the attention of her companions, Sister Agnes forced herself to take some food. When the meal was over she excused herself and went to her room.

The wound continued to hurt. It seemed as though the hand was being torn and the blood flowed through the hole. Each time as she looked, Sister Agnes thought of the seriousness of her sins and tried to bear the pain, recalling the sufferings of Christ on the cross. In her effort to remain calm, she tried to divert her attention by taking up her work, a crocheted handbag with little colored decorations. Pressing the crochet needle between the fingers of her left hand, stretched out with great pain, she began to work with an invocation at each movement of the needle. As a prayer she could only repeat, "Lord, have pity, forgive my offenses!"

How much time passed in this way? Suddenly, she jumped because the superioress tapped her on the shoulder. Sister Agnes was surprised because she thought the superioress had left with another sister and was not going to return to the convent until the next day.

Account of the Superioress:*

"That evening we had been invited to eat at a house in town and we were to spend the night in one of our convents there, but I was preoccupied by the condition of sister Agnes, so I decided to return to the convent. I went directly

---

*Father Yasuda refers to this superioress as Sister K., and refers to any other sisters in the community only by the first initial of their last name. Sister K. was not always the superioress throughout these events, but we continue to refer to her by this title as a means of identification.

to her room where I found her seated on her bed crocheting. At my request she opened her hand with great difficulty and said to me with tears in her eyes: 'It hurts me so that I took out my work.'

"She seemed in agony. 'If I have come to this, it is perhaps that my sins are grave?'

✏ "As for myself, I felt that this must have been sent to her by the Lord. 'It seems to hurt you very much, but try to bear it by thinking of the sufferings of the Lord. Excuse us for causing you to bear the consequences of the sins of us all.'

"I tried to console her as best I could and I went to look for one of the other sisters. The two of us treated the wound with gauze and bandaged the hand and asked her to awaken us if the pain increased, then we retired."

The Trial of Deafness, Source of Light

How did Sister Agnes pass that long night? She tells us:

"When my two companions had left my room wishing me goodnight, it was just 9 o'clock, the time when the community retires. Preparing myself as best I could for the night, I stretched out, but the pain was such that I was incapable of closing my eyes. I knelt down resting upon my heels. Squeezing the Rosary between my fingers, I begged the help of the Blessed Virgin and prayed as much as I could for the pardon of my sins. It came time to change the bandage because the wound was bleeding abundantly and at certain moments the pain doubled in intensity.

"I noticed something curious: the blood stopped some moments when I was drying it, which does not happen with ordinary wounds.

"But each time I tried to stretch out to sleep a little, the pain caused me to jump and I was obliged to remain seated to pray. Several times I tried in vain to find sleep when, softly, a thought took form within my heart like a ray of light piercing through the darkness: *What is the matter with you that you are so troubled?*

✔ "How could God send trials without meaning? I had learned in the course of the circumstances of my life that it is exactly at the time that one thinks one is doing well, filled with graces which come to be taken for granted, that a change comes like a cold shower to take us by surprise. The tasks which proceed well and make us proud, especially those which begin to preoccupy us, are taken away one day or the other...

"Likewise, when my ears suddenly became deaf in the church of Myoko, was not everything going splendidly? Was I not fulfilled by my new activities? And if it was not the height of success, was I not satisfied by the thought of a future which seemed brilliant?

"Certainly, when I had taken up my position as guardian at the church, I was disturbed by what awaited me. I had just left the hospital without any experience of society nor any particular preparation for being a catechist. Happily, the cooperation of those around me made my task easy. After having had my mother at my side for two weeks (she had hastened to the side of her daughter who didn't even know how to cook rice because she had been hospitalized a good part of her life), some attentive women of the parish brought me three meals each day for a month. The hospital was only three minutes away on foot, and I went each day to take my baths and I was received like a member of the family. Sick persons called me to their bedside one after the other to hear about the good God and had themselves baptized to the joy of the doctors and the nurses.

"Even when I was alone at the church I had nothing difficult to do. My purpose was to pray and be a humble servant of Mary and to live in the service of God and of the neighbor. One day when I was praying thus in the church someone knocked at the door: 'I would like to hear you speak of God.'

"Struck with joy at the sight of my first aspirant, I hastened to have her come in. And the word spread from person to person, mouth to mouth, and soon I found myself regularly with seven or eight persons during my hours of catechetical instruction.

"Only by the action of the Holy Spirit was I able to respond and attend to these persons seeking God while I had no theological knowledge, guiding myself simply by the aid of a precise Catholic doctrine. I told them, 'It is not theory that counts, *it is the joy of believing* that I would like to communicate to you. If I would be able, I would open wide the doors of my heart so that one would understand with an overwhelming joy far surpassing the sentences of a book.' Was prayer for my brethren stronger than persuasion? In any event, seventy persons received baptism from the time I had arrived at this church.

"Although I was well aware that I was not the cause of these graces, a feeling of satisfaction had taken hold of me. I felt myself more and more attached to my work. Was it not exactly because of that that the shock of deafness struck me?

"When I found myself suddenly plunged into the void of silence, lost in a stupor in the middle of the church with the Rosary squeezed in my fingers, I felt forming within me the words of Job crying from the depths of his misery: 'The Lord has given, the Lord has taken away, blessed be the name of the Lord!' And was not this my case? ... Ashamed of my failing faith and my lack of confidence, I began to shed warm tears. And after having wept a considerable time, an interior calm came over me as though my fate had finally touched bottom. Since such was His Will, what did it matter if I understood or did not understand? Should I not offer in praise all that He asked of me?...Enlightened by this powerful reflection, I felt an enthusiasm which caused me to understand, if I dare say so, what a martyr might experience. From that moment nothing more would be able to trouble me. If my neighbors would pity me in tears, I was at least able to keep my serenity.

"I can never forget the day when I had to say goodbye to the church in Myoko. After the last visits of friends and acquaintances, I went back for a last time, not without emotion, to look at the church which I would not see again. Large flakes of snow fell in silence and after a moment, soon wiped out the traces of my footsteps. Truly, my task at Myoko was over! Certainly I would be able to pray for the people I had known, but I must not look back on any success as my own. I was quite aware that *even the trace of my footsteps must disappear.*

"And now it was the same. I had become accustomed to the life in the convent on the hill and I had begun to hold my place in this little community. The Lord sent me a new

31.

trial. It was not so much the work that He willed from me. It seemed rather that He invited me to contemplate Him in order to progress into a more intimate union.

"I knew very well that it all depends on His Will. I had felt the effects of His grace which had permitted me to bear sufferings throughout my entire life. Therefore, why should I permit myself to be troubled?

"These thoughts which followed silently into my soul soon overcame my anguish. As a despairing person who has finally found a pillar to which to cling, it became much easier to bear the intense pain that continued to afflict my hand."

As we can see from the above reflections of Sister Agnes, it is clear that this event has a profound meaning in her spiritual development. At the same time, it is a part of that long development for the moment chosen by Mary to communicate important messages to the world.

The long struggle with suffering, the apparition of an angel in the form of a woman, the sudden loss of hearing, the mysterious light, the vision of the cohort of angels, the renewed apparition of the same heavenly person four years later who seems to be her guardian angel... all these surprising events have a coherent sequence and a profound meaning.

As everyone knows, the history of mystics in the Catholic Church offers numerous examples of saints who have received the stigmata which are painful wounds of the passion of Christ. Francis of Assisi and Catherine of Siena are among the more famous examples.

Sometimes, it also happens that persons who do not especially merit to be called saints receive the wounds of the Cross. The Church looks upon such phenomena with prudence and guards against hasty veneration of signs too rapidly attributed to Divine Grace.

In our time, such signs are considered more often as symptoms of mental disorders, such as hysteria. They are usually looked upon with doubt, if not with disdain.

Nevertheless we must discern, and one of the criteria of discernment of hysterical persons marked by this kind of wound is that they take a particular delight in showing it.

It is as if they had received a special distinction from Christ in Person and they would like all the world to know it.

The attitude of Sister Agnes is at all points opposed to what we have just said. From the moment she had this mysterious wound engraved in her hand, *she thought only of her own sins* and she applied herself, humble and confused, to hide the wound from those around her.

I dared to ask her later if she had not thought of the word "stigmata." Her response was simple, "Never in the world! I indeed had heard of stigmata, but are not such holy wounds reserved for the great saints like Saint Francis of Assisi who received them in a state of ecstasy during an apparition of Christ? How could I ever have thought for a second of so great a favor?"

For her part, the sister who found her in the room intuitively felt that the wound had been sent by the Lord. She felt impelled to console and to comfort Sister Agnes *who was ceaselessly lamenting her state of sinfulness*.

In the case of hysteria, it seems that the more painful the wound, the more it is accompanied by a feeling of delight and a tendency to brag about it. The subject needs to feel recognized because of vanity. There is nothing like this in the case of Sister Agnes. From the moment that she is aware of the phenomenon, the idea of her sins being the cause fills her with confusion. And when one asked her to which sins she referred, *it was a question only of very ordinary weaknesses* which are the sign of a delicate conscience (such as a lack of faith, insufficient gratitude, and so on).

It goes without saying, that this kind of extraordinary experience requires a great deal of prudence before concluding that it is of heavenly origin. One cannot see the Hand of God in just every extraordinary fact. Nevertheless, it is likewise wrong to jump to the conclusion that such an extraordinary event is the result of hysteria.

When one considers the road followed by Sister Agnes, her entire life and her spirituality, it becomes clear that this wound was a Divine intervention like the other phenomena which preceded it, and, as we shall see, it was to have a special meaning in the entire sequence of events leading up to a great message for the world.

33.

It seems that Sister Agnes was being purified in the crucible of a sequence of trials in order to be more attentive and more open for the communication the Mother of God was to make to the world through her.

And one can begin to understand the importance of those messages in the light of the painful and extraordinary preparations which preceded them.

†††

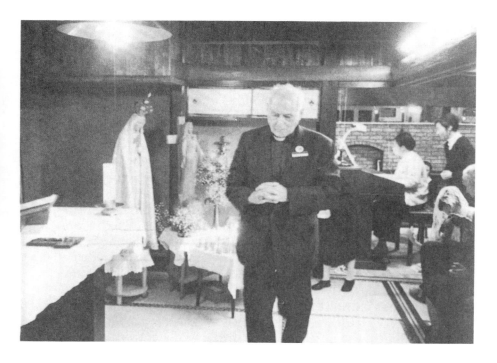

Above: Father John Engler, chaplain of the first organized pilgrimage to Akita from the U.S., returns after making act of consecration before the weeping Madonna. "Who can fail to be moved," he asks, "by our Mother's tears?" The statue of Our Lady of Fatima is the International Pilgrim Virgin which also shed tears. It was taken to Akita by the American group of the World Apostolate of Fatima led by Father Engler.

Chapter Four

The First Message of Mary

Returning back to that night of Thursday, July 5th: While bearing the piercing pain in her hand, Sister Agnes began to feel growing in her a greater abandonment to the Will of the Lord as she reflected on the meaning of all the trials of her life. The same prayer continued to rise to her lips, "Lord, have pity! Pardon my offenses!"

Tormented by the piercing pain, she was obliged to get up and to lie down without stopping, incapable of closing her eyes. It was already profound night when, towards 3 o'clock in the morning, she continues: "I had just changed the bandage again and was praying. Then I heard a voice which came from I know not where saying:

"'Do not fear. Pray with fervor not only because of your sins, but in reparation for those of all men. The world today wounds the most Sacred Heart of Our Lord by its ingratitudes and injuries. The wounds of Mary are much deeper and more sorrowful than yours. Let us go to pray together in the chapel.'

"While I had become a little accustomed to the angel, I had never looked at her face, as she always stood near my right shoulder. But now seeing her, I noticed such a striking resemblance to my elder sister that I instinctively called her by my sister's name. The latter had died some years before after having received the grace of Baptism.

"She smiled at me sweetly and made a light, negative movement of her head. She said: 'I am the one who is with you and watches over you.'

"At the same time, she beckoned me towards the chapel and disappeared from my eyes. I quickly dressed and went out to the corridor where I found her a few steps in front of me. I followed her along the corridor with rapid steps, filled with a sense of security comparable to that of a little child held by the hand. The moment I put my foot in the chapel she who had been so close to me like a reassuring presence, disappeared from my eyes. "Finding myself alone, I bowed in the direction of the altar and then turned towards the statue of the holy Virgin. The words of the angel resounded still in my soul, '*The wounds of Mary are much deeper and more sorrowful...* '

"At that time, the statue was placed on the right side of the altar. When I put my foot on the step of the altar, *I suddenly felt that the wooden statue came to life and was about to speak to me.* I looked: *She was bathed in a brilliant light.* Instinctively, I prostrated myself on the ground and at the same moment a voice of indescribable beauty struck my totally deaf ears:

"*'My daughter, my novice, you have obeyed me well in abandoning all to follow me. Is the infirmity of your ears painful? Your deafness will be healed, be sure. Be patient. It is the last trial. Does the wound of your hand cause you to suffer? Pray in reparation for the sins of men. Each person in this community is my irreplaceable daughter. Do you say well the prayer of the Handmaids of the Eucharist? Then, let us pray it together.'*

"As this beautiful voice began the prayer, the angel who had led me to the chapel reappeared at my side and joined in. Always prostrate and thinking of nothing else, I had just said the words, '*Jesus present in the Eucharist,*' when the voice interrupted me, adding: '*Truly present.*' And to impress this all the more upon my troubled spirit, the voice added: '*From now on, you will add TRULY*'"

(In the prayer composed by the Bishop for the Institute of the Handmaids of the Eucharist, the words originally were simply: "Jesus present in the Eucharist.")

"Did I even have the time to answer yes? All I know is that I thought only of uniting myself to that voice of such inexpressible beauty which seemed to come from Heaven. I was aided also by the sweet voice of the angel speaking by my side. Our three voices together prayed:

"*Most Sacred Heart of Jesus, truly present in Holy Eucharist, I consecrate my body and soul to be entirely one with Your Heart, being sacrificed at every instant on all the altars of the world and giving praise to the Father pleading for the coming of His Kingdom.*

"*Please receive this humble offering of myself. Use me as You will for the glory of the Father and the salvation of souls.*

"*Most Holy Mother of God, never let me be separated from Your Divine Son. Please defend and protect me as Your special child. Amen.*

"When the prayer was finished, the Heavenly Voice* said:

"'*Pray very much for the Pope, Bishops and Priests. Since your Baptism you have always prayed faithfully for them. Continue to pray very much... very much. Tell your superior all that passed today and obey him in everything that he will tell you. He has asked that you pray with fervor.*'

"After a short moment of silence, the angel began a familiar prayer. I at once said it with her: 'Lord Jesus Christ, Son of the Father.' When this prayer was over I timidly raised my head. The luminous splendor had completely disappeared. The angel was no longer visible and the statue had resumed its normal aspect."

In the above account, it is fitting that we should note first of all the declaration of the celestial "guide." To show that she is not an illusion, she begins by denying absolutely that she is Sister Agnes' elder sister (as she had presumed) and she identifies herself, "*I am the one who is with you and who watches over you.*" That is to say, it is clearly the guardian angel whose existence is taught to us in Catechism. Therefore, we will use this title in the rest of the account.

It is touching to see Sister Agnes look at the angel for the first time (now a little accustomed to having her appear) and to hear escape from her lips the name of her sister. Rather than a physical resemblance, it is perhaps the feeling of the sweet and protective presence her sister had always had for her which awakened this reaction.

This elder sister had succumbed to a cancer of the stomach eight years before Sister Agnes arrived at the convent at Yuzawadai. Sister Agnes and her mother had taken care of her during her hospitalization. At the request of the husband, Sister Agnes spoke to her of God, after which the sister was baptized. As she knew she was going to die and leave behind three young children, she asked Sister Agnes to replace her as mother and spouse. Agnes

---

*As we shall see shortly, *this was the voice of Our Lady.*

Then had to make known to her that she wished to be consecrated to the Lord in thanksgiving for all graces received. The elder sister understood immediately and acceded to her request, "When you are in heaven, you will pray that I will be able to enter the convent." And Agnes added, "If I am accepted, that will mean that you are in heaven... "

Before the cancer, the elder sister had always been in robust health and had always taken care of Agnes who, as we know, had been delicate from earliest childhood. She discreetly saw that Agnes was spared physical works imposed by relatives who were accustomed to strict discipline. In the good as well as the bad moments, she had always surrounded her younger sister with attentive affection.

When one considers all these circumstances, it is not surprising that Sister Agnes first thought she saw her deceased sister in the comforting apparition of the angel.

Indeed, when we asked Sister Agnes to describe the face of the angel she could give us only vague explanations, "A round face, an expression of sweetness..." As for the garments, she could only say, "A person covered with a shining whiteness like snow..."

She added that this brightness is nothing comparable to the luminous splendor which emanated from the statue of Mary when she heard Her voice. That brightness was so intense that she immediately prostrated herself. She was incapable of saying whether the face of Our Lady had changed expression in the course of the vision because she could not lift her head, so deeply was she moved. What then could she tell us about the voice of Mary?

This seems to be what is most difficult to describe. In her effort to try to express as much as possible the beauty of this voice, Sister Agnes often uses an expression which in her dialect means, "of a beauty without limit."

One day, I was speaking with a stranger who had come to the convent on the recommendation of Bishop Ito and we were speaking again of the voice. "A voice never heard and which certainly could not have come from this world," Sister tried to explain while seeking just the right expression since the stranger asked, "Was it comparable to that of the angel?" Sister Agnes replied, "The two voices are beautiful, but the voice of Mary has something more divine."

"Can you explain this difference by comparison?"

She reflected a moment and then said, "One can say that the voice of the angel resembles a song and that of Mary, a prayer."

The stranger seemed overcome with this answer. "It is a very beautiful comparison. I understand much better now."

But let us take up again our account of the events. The statue was again in its normal state and then Sister Agnes remembered that she wanted to observe the condition of the hand. She was about to get up when she noticed that a sister was now praying next to her. *It was already ten minutes after five in the morning,* although she thought it was still in the middle of the night (because she had left her room about three o'clock in the morning). But the hour of Lauds was approaching and her companions were arriving in the chapel one after the other.

After Lauds, Sister Agnes decided to ask the superioress to look at the statue for her, but as they were getting ready to leave for Mass, it did not seem to be the fitting moment. She preferred to wait, and got into the car with the others, taking care not to draw attention to the state of her own hand.

As the convent was without a priest even on the First Friday of the month, they were obliged to go into town or to a neighboring community to assist at Mass.

When they came back to the hill, Sister Agnes did not have the courage to go to look at the statue herself. In reality, the more the time passed, the more her anguish increased at the idea that there might be something there. She had less and less desire to approach it, held back by a sentiment of veneration and fear. Finally, she asked the Mistress of Novices to go to see whether or not there was a wound on the hand of the Virgin. She was troubled about speaking to anyone before speaking first to the Bishop, but she felt it proper to ask the Mistress of Novices, whom the Bishop himself had appointed to guide her in the course of her Novitiate. And if she wanted to refer this to the Bishop later, it would first be proper to make sure of the facts. She waited some time in her room, but the sister did not come. After a considerable time, Sister Agnes decided to go to the chapel to see what had happened.

Alone before the statue of Mary, the Mistress was on her knees with joined hands. When she perceived the presence of Sister Agnes, she turned toward her, her eyes filled with tears, signaling her to advance closer, and pointed her finger in the direction of the right hand of the statue. Sister Agnes approached, looked, and then immediately prostrated herself on the ground as though struck by an electric charge.

It was true! There was a wound in the middle of the little hand made of wood. Two lines crossed each other and *blood flowed from the central hole*, creating a most sorrowful spectacle.

What indeed could that mean? Overcome by a fear mixed with respect, Sister Agnes could not even weep. The words heard during the night came back to her, "Pray in reparation for the sins of men." She said to herself, "Is the wound of Mary due to the sadness because of ingratitudes and outrages of man? Does She show Her pain in order to incite us to conversion and penance? It is the time to confide to Her everything and to place oneself entirely with Her in prayer!"

"Here is a visible and undoubtable sign, it is best to tell the others, it is even necessary... " said the Novice Mistress.

Soon another sister came and prostrated.

That evening, the event was told to the sisters as they returned to the convent from their different works. They asked Sister Agnes to show her own wound, which she did with docility, extending her painful hand. She said only, "Would you please pray for me who am a sinner?"

It is important to realize that pain had prevented Sister Agnes from sleeping during the night. She was completely awake, physically and psychologically, and in full possession of reason and lucidity. The words exchanged with the angel and her going to the chapel at the angel's direction, are described with clear detail, as are the transformation of the statue shining with a divine light, and the words pronounced by a voice whose sweetness was without comparison, inviting her to pray the prayer of the Handmaids of the Eucharist.

All the above excludes the possibility that Sister Agnes might have been in a state of semi-sleep. Furthermore, one can say that the wound in the form of a cross on the right hand of the statue authenticates the supernatural character of the facts, showing this to be, indeed, an intervention from Heaven. In the years during which these events were subjected to intense and sometimes hostile scrutiny, there was talk of hallucination, somnambulism and of ectoplasmic phenomena.

However, as one can see from all that has already passed, and as one is to see in all that follows, Sister Agnes was not touched by this kind of anomaly. The lengthy and profound tests to which she submitted at the Faculty of Medicine of Akita rule out such speculations.

The unexpected greeting of the Virgin from the transformed statue constitutes in some way the first step toward the important messages to follow. Mary prepares Her instrument for the essential part of Her message, in order that she might not be too much disconcerted by what is to follow. She thanks her for having offered her life, shows concern for the pain of her deafness, consoles her and finally guides her in prayer while showing the example. Does not one feel that in all this Our Lady is showing the solicitude of Her Immaculate Heart?

Testimonies Concerning July 6th

Testimony of the Novice Mistress

"On that day Sister Agnes must have risen earlier than usual because she was prostrate before the statue of Mary when I arrived in the chapel. Later, when I returned from the city where we had assisted at Mass in a convent, she met me at the door and asked:

"'Could you go to see if something has changed on the statue of the Blessed Virgin? I was told something this morning about this and I am concerned.' I went at once to the chapel and when I came before the statue of Mary sculptured in wood I saw a blackish mark on the palm of the right hand in the form of a cross. One would have said that it had been traced with a fine point of a pencil about 1.5 centimeters high and 1.3 centimeters wide. It is to be remarked that the wound seemed actually bigger in the small hand of the statue which is only 70 centimeters high. I at once remembered that I am only a sinner and I prostrated myself weeping, asking pardon aloud.

"While I was doing this, Sister Agnes came, wondering why I had not returned. I showed her at once the condition of the hand and she seemed to be seized with fear and astonishment. A short time afterwards I called Sister T. K. to look. Then I asked them to keep silent about it.

"I returned to the chapel to pray several times and about 3 o'clock in the afternoon I saw that the blood which had flowed from the wound had dried and I went to inform Sister Agnes and Sister T. K.

"When another sister returned from town I explained everything to her and took her to see the statue. She asked me if the statue had not always been like that and I assured her there had been nothing there. Of course I knew because I had painted a picture of the statue over a period of two months, in the course of which I had been able to observe it at leisure down to the smallest detail.

"Those who saw the phenomenon for the first time, including Sister T. K., seemed to have some doubts and hesitated about what attitude to take. All the sisters came to observe the statue one after the other, but since it was forbidden to speak about it among ourselves the question was not brought up during dinner that day. Indeed if it were truly a grace come from Heaven (a miracle) any light conversation risked soiling the mystery..."

Witness of Sister T. K.

"The Novice Mistress of Sister Agnes told me: 'There is a wound in the form of a cross on the right hand of the statue of Mary. I have not yet spoken to the Bishop, but do not fail to go and see now,' which I did immediately. There was indeed a wound in the form of a cross on the right hand of the statue. The lateral branch was 1.6 centimeters and the vertical branch was 1.7 centimeters. One would have said that they were traced by a pen with black ink. On these lines there stood out two darker points. It resembled very much ink which had spread under the effect of heat. I said to myself that the Novice Mistress must have spoken of these points when she saw blood flow through a hole as large as that of a needle.

"Considered with the eyes of nature, it resembled something traced with a pen. However, when one contemplated it with the look of faith, one felt a profound feeling of peace. Ordinarily I am very careful about physical observation of facts, but here it was faith which carried me away and forced me to my knees, prostrate in prayer.

"I returned to the refectory and then returned to the chapel a half hour or an hour later and knelt before the statue of Mary. This time the hand had a clearly different aspect. The height of the cross was the same as before but instead of appearing like ink out of a pen, it seemed to be truly cut into the flesh. *The edge of the cross had the aspect of human flesh and one even saw the grain of the skin like a fingerprint. I said to myself at that moment that the wound was real.* I was deeply impressed and I felt in the depth of myself that this metamorphosis was a warning of Mary in view of my still undecided attitude.

"That day the wound underwent several transformations. Sister K. having told me that blood had flowed from it, I hastened to see the statue. Some blood flowed down as if it was coming forth from the wound, having impregnated the wood. I said to myself that blood impregnated in the wood must indeed give that color."

Testimony of Sister Y. I.

"The First Friday of July when I returned from the school where I worked, towards six o'clock in the evening, Sister K. told me about the wound which appeared on the hand of the statue of the Blessed Virgin.

"Approaching the statue I saw in the middle of the palm of the right hand that a wound in the form of a cross had been cut with something like the tip of a blade. It was about 1.5 centimeters by 2 centimeters. I can certify that such a mark did not exist there before. I was in charge of the sacristy for five years and I often had occasion to clean the statue. There was no possibility of error.

"That evening, in the chapel, I asked Sister Agnes to show me again the wound in her left hand. There were two red traces in the form of a cross and they seemed to cause her pain."

Bishop Ito, speaking at the U.S. National Center of the Blue Army in Washington, N.J., in June, 1988 on his return from Rome where he spoke with Cardinal Ratzinger about his pastoral letter approving Akita. "I was very pleased," the Bishop said, "with the Cardinal's response."

Chapter Five

The Following Days

It was natural that the sisters would now give additional attention to Sister Agnes. That she had received a mysterious wound in the hand was already known, and she alone had been the one affected. And now *the same wound* in the form of the cross *had appeared on the wooden statue of Mary.*

Reduced to silence by word of the Bishop, each sister was at the same time careful to treat Sister Agnes in a perfectly normal way. They showed a new fervor in prayer, sustained by a more filial love towards Mary to the degree that they progressed in silent meditation.

Each time Sister Agnes would think again of the sad aspect of the wound on the statue of Our Lady, she felt herself overcome in the deepest part of her being and preoccupied as to the meaning of this phenomenon. But she felt somewhat relieved with regard to the bitter reproaches she had heaped upon herself.

We now come to the following Thursday, July 12th. When Sister K. arrived at the chapel for the evening office, two sisters praying in front of the statue signaled for her to come and look at the hand.

"The hand of the Blessed Virgin is bleeding again. Look at the palm. It is still humid."

Blood seemed to have just flowed forming a line leading from the center of the hand down to the little finger, where it stopped. The shock felt was no less than it had been the preceding time.

During the evening prayer, the wound of Sister Agnes began again to pain her.

The following day, Friday the 13th, the whole community went into the city to assist at Mass. After having conducted their courses, they returned to the hill toward midday. They wanted to go into the chapel, but when they found that the door had been locked by two mistresses who had gone out to work and had taken the keys, they were obliged to recite the Angelus in the refectory.

The door of the chapel was opened by Sister K. when she returned for the evening office. To their amazement they found that the blood was flowing again from the hand of Mary. Seen close up, it appeared to have just begun streaming to the end of the little finger. The repetition of this phenomenon, so sad to see, only caused the apprehension of Sister Agnes to increase, overcome as she was by the original shock of the wound.

The first time, a week earlier, even though she had been alerted by the angel, Sister Agnes had fallen prostrate under such emotion that she had doubted what she saw. The same experience being repeated two or three times, she was as overcome by each as by the first. It was not one of those isolated events to which one becomes accustomed after awhile. A wound appearing on the hand of a person is nothing in comparison. But this prodigious sign, which defied all laws of nature... what indeed could it mean? Surely *something urgent and serious* was indicated.

Sister Agnes did everything possible so that no one would know the anguish and the emotion that troubled her heart. She paid special attention to fulfilling her daily tasks while she did not cease to pray in silence, *"Lord, have pity, have pity on us!"*

Strange to relate, the wound which did not hurt her so much on the other days always began to torment her on Thursday night, the pain continuing throughout Friday, the following day. Thus on July 19th, the following Thursday, piercing pain occurred in the evening and was so violent on Friday, that she was unable to take up her work at sewing and could not participate in the kitchen work which wet the hands. On Saturday the wound remained, but the pain had ceased.

Report to the Bishop

On July 24th, after a month of absence, the Bishop came for a visit. Having received the usual greetings from Sister K., he said quietly to Sister Agnes who brought him tea, "How are you?" Then he heard the account made to him by Sister K. of the events which had taken place since his previous visit and he told Sister Agnes to show him her hand. A little disturbed for not having spoken to the Bishop about this a month sooner, she nevertheless braced herself and opened her palm to his view.

It was a Tuesday. The wound appeared a little smaller but one clearly saw the form of the cross. The Bishop removed his glasses and looked carefully, then without saying a word he went to the chapel with Sister K. to take account of the condition of the statue.

At 4 o'clock in the afternoon he called Sister Agnes to listen in detail about the events that took place during his absence. She made a faithful and detailed account beginning with what had happened to her personally and ending up with the prodigy of the statue. Aided by a good memory and by notes taken during those days, she was agreeably surprised to be able to make a precise and detailed account.

It is especially astonishing that she had written under the strain of emotion, driven by an interior force, so that every detail was accurately recalled. And one cannot fail to see in this once again the mysterious intervention of a helping hand.

The following day the Bishop celebrated the Mass followed by an hour of adoration. Then Sister Agnes was called again. The Bishop asked her to begin from the beginning and repeat everything to the end. She did so repeating exactly the same details. (When one answers questions in complete loyalty and good faith, without additions or subtractions, it goes without saying that one can repeat the same thing ten times without making a mistake).

The Bishop made no commentary. He merely repeated the same recommendation made in his preceding visit: "Be careful not to say to yourself: It is a phenomenon especially destined for me. I am a special case. Strive for humility."

Sister Agnes who listened with deference, experienced great confusion, as her testimony shows: "How could I have imagined being a special case? I have no special gift and furthermore my infirmity renders me incapable of doing the work of a person not handicapped. All the others are considered as teachers when they go out because they have a diploma or a particular qualification. But I, I do not even have a catechist certificate and I am capable only of taking charge of a chapel. I thought that it was just because of my sins that this penance had been given to me and that it was rather normal.

"Also, when the Bishop told me that I should not become proud because of it, my only desire was to throw myself at his feet and to beg him with all my strength to pray for the poor sinner that I am. Taking my courage by both hands I asked him to please continue to direct and pray for me. He answered me with these kind words, 'Very well, it is understood.'

"I left the room perfectly comforted and truly thankful. Further, the more I thought about it the more I realized that from the beginning of these events, despite a tendency to blame everything on my personal sins, I felt my soul filled with an interior peace which was like a comforting light. That, too, was certainly a grace received... "

Once again it is to be noted that Sister Agnes thought everything was due to her sins and she never imagined for a moment that the same wound could appear on the statue of the Virgin. If she had not been prepared so well by the announcement of the angel, the shock most probably would have plunged her into extreme confusion. The announcement made by the angel seems to have a deep meaning which does not concern only Sister Agnes:

"Do not pray only because of your sins, but in reparation for the sins of all men. The world today, by its ingratitude and outrages, wounds the most Sacred Heart of Our Lord. The wound on the hand of Mary is much deeper and more painful than yours."

Up to this time Sister Agnes alone had received the signs, whether the light from the tabernacle or the vision of the angels in adoration. This time, the signs became public after the angel led her to the chapel where she received the unexpected greeting before the statue of Our Lady. More and more the entire community was becoming involved and drawn into deeper prayer and reparation.

Again one sees beyond the individual appeal an urgency whose meaning is universal: "Pray in reparation for all men... pray especially for the Pope, the Bishops and the Priests... " This invitation appears as the prologue to the urgent warning which will soon follow, emphasized by the wound in the center of the hand of Our Lady's statue.

This wound was a tangible prodigy visible to all believers and nonbelievers. It was a mysterious sign produced to authenticate in a manifest way the supernatural origin of the message received.

It is not at all surprising that forgetting her personal sufferings Sister Agnes exclaimed with an anguished cry: "It is certainly something serious!"

She relates the development of her reaction from that moment: "My heart which until then had been closed with thoughts which hardly went beyond the fear of sin seemed to be enlarged and purified by this new sign. From now on my companions shared with me the burden which had become almost insupportable and which now became bearable."

It is true that she alone heard the angel and the Virgin. And anyone might have said that these were just her own ideas. But the phenomenon of the wound in the hand of Our Lady, which had been announced by the angel, was now clearly and beyond any doubt revealed to the eyes of all.

Naturally when the news was first published in Japan, those who can judge only by natural laws sought every kind of explanation. But the power of God surpasses human knowledge. Saint Luke recalls to us in Verse 37, Chapter 1: "Nothing is impossible to God." When His Force manifests itself in defiance of physical laws, one says that it is a miracle. Even when it cannot be understood by human standards, it is there before the eyes of men as an undeniable reality.

Furthermore, when a message seems to be given by Heaven it must be in conformity to the teaching of Scriptures, as is the case here. As for the miracle, it is given as an objective sign which confirms the supernatural origin of the message. In the case of the statue of Akita, everything happened without the least human intervention.

To deny this, it was proposed that Sister Agnes had ectoplasmic powers. According to this theory she was able in some way to transfer her own wound onto the wood and to transfer to it her own blood. This thesis was constructed and published without any inquiry ever having been made at Yuzawadai itself. (As we shall see later, the analysis of the blood from the statue showed that it was *not* from Sister Agnes!)

Let us not forget that Sister Agnes was totally deaf when she clearly received the words of the Angel and of Mary. Trained to read lips, she could converse in daily life every day, but her ears were closed to every kind of sound and so much the more to human voices. Showing a natural facility to decipher words even without seeming to keep her eyes riveted on the lips of the person speaking to her, she was finally able to talk like everyone in such a way that sometimes one would forget her infirmity and turn one's back while continuing to speak to her, which of course caused her to lose the thread of the conversation. The movement of the lips was for her the only detectable sign of speech.

But those "beautiful voices" of the celestial world were very truly heard by her ears. It seems that she had been able to communicate independently of physical conditions necessary in normal times, namely by the vibrations of the air and of the eardrum.

In the face of all this what were the reactions of her own companions, her own sisters? All the testimony cited earlier shows the same amazement, mixed with veneration as well as an application of this to oneself as would be understandable for religious persons. Even though they are religious, they are human beings endowed with reason like everyone and one can easily understand the trouble and the doubts they experienced at the beginning.

Sister I., eldest member of the Institute and close to the director, Bishop Ito, possessed a rich culture, matured by a long experience of life. When she went to look at the state of the statue at the first news, she did not seem to be very moved. Then suddenly, her two hands joined, she fell prostrate saying in a strong voice, "My Lord and my God!," which quite surprised the community.

Later she explained her reaction. At the very moment that she thought that she was the victim of a bad joke (someone had surely amused themselves by making marks with a pen) some *blood came forth* from a little central hole.

Instinctively she repeated the cry of St. Thomas. As the disciple doubting the resurrected Christ Who had to show him His wounds, she felt a strong emotion mixed with fear and veneration. Other sisters had a similar experience.

There is no way one can consider as hallucination or optical illusion a fact thus verified by several persons both simultaneously and at different times. It was not an instantaneous and passing event because it was able to be verified several times over during the same day. Various changes of more or less importance were observed each time as if the wound *were alive*. The silence imposed by the superior was a wise measure nevertheless. Every supernatural phenomenon does not necessarily come from God. Could it be the action of some other mysterious force? It was not a matter to be treated lightly.

Nevertheless, they were all aware in their minds and hearts that this was not a simple event destined to fall into oblivion after having astonished a few naive religious. They silently shared the apprehension of Sister Agnes:

"It is surely something important!"

The Strange Phenomena Increase

Thursday, the 26th of July, was the Feast of Saint Ann, the mother of the Virgin Mary. In the afternoon during the 5 o'clock Mass Sister Y.I. was to renew her vows. Sister Agnes who had been for sometime appointed as her spiritual counselor was happy to be able to share with her so great a joy.

It was past 3 o'clock when Sister S.I. came to the room with Sister Agnes to say that she could not find Sister K. anywhere. Sister Agnes thought at once to look in the chapel. They went there and found Sister K. kneeling before the statue of Mary between the Bishop and Sister I. They were reciting the Rosary. After a moment of hesitation, Sister Agnes advanced to tell Sister K. that she was expected.

The Sister turned, her eyes full of tears: "The blood flows again from the hand of Mary. Today there is much more, and it has a somber color which makes it painful to see. Take my place," she said, leaving.

It was not necessary to come any closer to be struck by the presence not of a thread but of a large stain of blood in the center of the hand. Sister Agnes could not approach the Bishop and took a step backward. "Such a quantity of blood! What does it mean?"

Sister I. turned towards her and asked her to join them in the Rosary. Hardly had they begun to pray when the wound of Sister Agnes' left hand jerked in pain. The other times it was always from Thursday evening and she was wondering why she had pain so soon. Despite it she forced herself to participate as well as she could in the prayers.

The Mass began after 5 o'clock. At the moment when Sister Y.I. read her Act of Consecration, the pain in Sister Agnes' hand reached an intensity never before known. The piercing was so strong that a cry escaped from her, although immediately repressed. It was as though a large drill transpierced the hand all the way through. It was followed by a bleeding. She held herself up, but from her forehead there appeared a heavy sweat... "Holy Mary, come to my help!" Having no other recourse than to clasp the medal which she wore at her neck, she united herself with all her soul to the sufferings of Jesus on the Cross. The moments of most insupportable pain were certainly of short duration, but the suffering she endured seemed interminable.

That evening she was appointed to say the first part of the prayers. This required from her a supreme effort which she tried to hide. Always sustained by the thought of the passion of Our Lord she fulfilled her task as best she could, but at the end her body was bathed in perspiration.

That evening the dinner had a festive air in honor of Sister Y.I. and Sister Agnes ate like everyone else in order not to cast a shadow on that happy day, hiding her hand which pained her greatly although not as violently as it had in the chapel.

After dinner she was summoned by the Bishop. She told him of the sharp pain which had tormented her during the Mass. When she tried to open her fingers she again experienced an incredible piercing pain. The Bishop observed the palm which she opened with great difficulty: "Oh! That must pain you very much. The wound risks passing from one side to the other... " The Bishop showed his great solicitude.

That evening as on the night of the First Friday of the month, she could not close her eyes the entire night. She sat on her bed, recited the Rosary, straightened the room while protecting her hand. She had to move constantly in order to bear the pain.

Dawn came like a deliverer. She hastened to the chapel, her only refuge. She participated in Lauds concentrating as best she could, but with a feeble voice.

During the Mass at 7 o'clock, at the Consecration, the pain again reached its zenith. Blood flowed. It seemed that the piercing reached such an extreme that it was as if the hand had been pierced through.

After the Mass which to her seemed interminable, she left the chapel and looked at her hand. There was a rather large quantity of blood. She did not dry it and went to show the Bishop. On the way she met Sister Y.I. who observed the wound with a sad expression.

One may wonder if the wound which appeared on the hand of the statue was exactly the same as that of Sister Agnes. In her intimate journal she states: "It was exactly the same wound in the form of a cross with blood which flowed from the center. However, since the statue had a hand much smaller its cross was smaller. The central opening was about as large as the hole of a sewing needle. Mine was much bigger, like the thickness of a drill. In the most painful moments one would have said that a serrated drill was twisting in the flesh and piercing through to the other side. It is then that the blood began to flow, but it caused so much pain that I did not have the strength to dry it. All that I could do was to pass a gauze between my fingers to sponge it.

"Strangely, the blood that appeared on the hand of the statue never fell to the ground. Even when Sister K. (kneeling with Sister I. and the Bishop) had alerted me with tears in her voice about the bleeding, the blood always remained in the palm of the statue even though the statue's hand is open and pointing downward... Furthermore, in my case also I felt that the blood accumulated when I prayed in the chapel but it never soiled the floor a single time. It is also strange that my wound did not open and did not twitch with pain except from Thursday to Friday. When the pain reached its peak on the 26th, the Bishop advised me to go to the hospital if it got worse. But on Saturday I no longer felt pain. The central orifice had only a rose color, but perhaps that was an impression."

TRANSLATOR'S NOTE:

We wish to call the reader's attention once more to the fact that Father Yasuda compiled this book from notes which he made over a period of two years. Because he was the chaplain of the convent, and because he was charged with the responsibility of recording all of these events by Bishop Ito, he sees fit to interrupt the narrative from time to time with important observations. These are usually set off from the rest of the text by the spacing breaks used below. And while Father Yasuda speaks so often of the providential signs, one must be impressed by the fact that Father Yasuda himself was most providential in this entire matter and indeed by extraordinary circumstances came to the convent of Yuzawa-dai. Seen in this light his comments, like those following, take on a very special meaning.

It is not rare for stigmatists to suffer the wounds only on Thursdays and Fridays, days of the week which recall the passion of Our Lord. On Saturday the pain would disappear exactly as it came, but it had been indeed felt like a cruel reality. "Never will I forget that pain," Sister Agnes recalls, repressing a shiver of fright.

Thus during the morning of the First Friday she went back to her room to divert her attention and thus attenuate the pain, but nothing helped, not reading, not even her dear crocheting. The time of suffering passed only in the contemplation of the Cross and meditation on the Passion of Our Lord.

During the free time of the afternoon she tried to give a little rest to her body deprived of sleep for two days. But the pain took over; lying or standing, she could not remain in one place. At 2:30 in the afternoon she was pierced with a pain of unheard of violence. Unable to bear more, she fled to the chapel as to her only refuge. Floored by pain, Sister Agnes prostrated herself.

Immediately the voice of the angel sounded to the ears of her heart:

*"Your sufferings will end today. Carefully engrave in the depth of your heart the thought of the blood of Mary. The blood shed by Mary has a profound meaning. This precious blood was shed to ask your conversion, to ask for peace, in reparation for the ingratitude and the outrages towards the Lord. As with devotion to the Sacred Heart, apply yourself to devotion to the most Precious Blood. Pray in reparation for all men."**

In her pain and surprise, Sister Agnes could not reply. The angel continued:

"Say to your superior that the blood is shed today for the last time. Your pain also ends today. Tell them what happened today. He will understand all immediately. And you, observe his directions." The angel ended with a smile and disappeared.

Sister Agnes regretted not having spoken to the angel. She noted that the pain in her hand had vanished at the same time that the angel disappeared... a pain so violent which ceased as though by magic without any trace of wound or blood, as though it were another hand!

Quickly she looked at the statue: from the hand of the statue blood still flowed through the hole. She was oppressed with a feeling of reproach regarding herself and did not feel daring enough to go closer to examine it. She left the sister who was praying beside her and returned to her room. While she was passing the entrance she was told that a rug which had been ordered for some time had just been delivered. She helped carry it up to the first floor with the service sister. They were spreading the carpet in the room upstairs when the one who had been praying in the chapel arrived. When she found herself alone with Sister Agnes she informed her that some blood had begun again to flow from the statue.

"I had taken a little on my index finger to show it to the Bishop but behold it disappeared while helping you here. Now it is no longer worthwhile to go."

---

*For an explanation of the relationship of "the blood of Mary" and the Precious Blood see the booklet *The Meaning of Akita*.

Sister Agnes was disturbed by this. She reproached herself for not having gone at once to inform the Bishop but since his Excellency remained in his room working, it did not seem proper to go to interrupt him to speak of their lack of vigilance. That day she kept the excuses to herself and did not go to see him.

It goes without saying that each one reacts differently with regard to the bleeding of the statue. Even though they share the same faith, some prostrate themselves, mute through sentiment of fear and veneration before the mystery; others pressed by a positive spirit seized the hand between their fingers to examine it more closely. For example, Sister I. took out a large magnifying glass and observed the wound minutely. Certainly such an attitude can be explained by her responsibility, but Sister Agnes, for her part would have been totally incapable of this. And so much the more it would be inconceivable for her, even for a single instant, to be so daring as to take some of the blood upon her finger.

"I do that! I have too much fear," she said shrugging her head down to her shoulders.

In order to well understand what she means we must understand that the word "fear" is used here in a special sense of Sister Agnes' regional dialect. For example if one must meet a person of elevated state, one will say: "But I am too much afraid to approach so illustrious a person." This does not mean fear in the common sense of the word but rather a sentiment of great respect. Also the frequent use of this word denotes in Sister Agnes what we might call the fear of God. After she knew that some blood of the statue had disappeared while they were putting down the carpet, she cleaned it with very special care.

One of the seven gifts of the Holy Spirit is the Fear of God. It seems that Sister Agnes had it in abundance!

Witnesses

Testimony of Sister Y. I.
with Regard to the Blood of the Statue

"What I remember best happened on Thursday, the 26th

of July, about 2 o'clock in the afternoon while I was arranging flowers on the altar for Mass. Something which looked like a large clot of dark blood was on the hand of the statue which had not been there before. I at once notified Sister T. K. who was in the kitchen in order that she might come and verify it. About 3 o'clock we called the Bishop so that he could see.

"On Friday, the 27th of July in the morning, I saw Sister Agnes showing her hand to the Bishop, ('Look at all this blood!') I had come upon them by accident and only saw the bandage which was soaked with it. One could see that it was fresh blood. During all the month of July the wound seemed to hurt her especially on Thursday evening and on Friday. According to what she said it was like a serrated drill which transpierced her hand and caused it to bleed to such an extent that she was dispensed from clearing the table after meals."

One remarks that the blood does not flow in streams but that it accumulates and that the wound of Sister Agnes causes her unbearable pain and is followed by rather an abundant hemorrhage. As is already indicated by the form of a cross, these phenomena show integral relation with the passion of Christ. They suggest the importance of an active participation (compassion) in the sacrifice of the cross, not only by thought but even to the point of sharing in the physical pain of Christ's suffering. This experience teaches us the necessity of offering all suffering of our daily life in union with the passion of Jesus.

When the guardian angel appears to the Sister while she is prostrate in the chapel at the end of her strength, the angel comforts her in drawing her attention to the meaning of the blood, "Carefully engrave in the depth of your heart the thought of the blood of Mary," she counsels Sister and then explains, "This precious blood has been shed to ask your conversion, to ask for peace, in reparation for the ingratitudes and the outrages toward the Lord..."

By the prodigy of blood flowing from a wooden statue, God manifests that the pain of Mary Conceived Without Sin is so profound that She sheds blood because of it.

When Mary presented the Infant Jesus in the Temple forty days after His Birth, almost 2000 years ago, the just

57.

Simeon prophesied: "This Child will be a sign of contradiction, and a sword will pierce your heart." (Luke 2, 34) In agreement with this prophecy, at the moment She assisted at the death of Her Son, standing at the foot of the cross, She felt Her soul "transpierced with a sword." All the sins of men committed from the beginning are the cause of the suffering of the Son of God on the cross. Likewise today there is a close link between these three: our sins, the suffering of the Crucified, and the suffering of the heart of Mary... a suffering unto the suffering of blood. That is why the angel recalls our attention once more to the profound meaning of the blood of Mary.

For her part Sister Agnes feels within her body an unheard of pain never before known, the experience of which is engraved in her memory. The wound whose opening is not larger than the passage of a toothpick causes her to break out into a heavy sweat. What must have been the sufferings of Him whose two feet were fixed to the wood by nails the thickness of a little finger?

The experience of Sister Agnes reminds us in a very vivid way of the need to meditate on the sufferings of Jesus agonizing on the gibbet of the cross and the sorrows which transpierced the heart of Mary. *It is a pressing appeal to respond by praise and changing of life to share the sacrifice of expiation in which Mary participated at the foot of the cross.*

Is that not the full meaning of this event? The angel gives the following interpretation, *"This precious blood has been shed in reparation for the ingratitude and the outrages committed against the Lord."* It is not a question only of sins committed by non-Christians, but perhaps above all because of the attitude of us Christians who so often abuse Divine grace. Then she announces that "the blood is shed today for the last time," after which, as though to console Sister Agnes, she repeats with a smile that Sister Agnes' sufferings will end this same day.

It all happened as the angel said. The trace of the wound was still visible on the statue for two months but blood no longer flowed from it. The wound of Sister Agnes disappeared and the pain vanished on the 27th of July without leaving the least trace.

Padre Pio, of the Capuchin Order in Italy, was among the great stigmatists of our century. His two hands, his two feet and his side bled exactly like the five wounds of Christ. But every trace of the wounds was effaced immediately after his death to the great astonishment of all. Photos taken ten minutes after his death showed the surface skin smooth and white on his feet and hands. If the wound of Sister Agnes is much less impressive, it nevertheless presents the same particularity of having appeared and disappeared in an absolutely involuntary and mysterious manner.

TRANSLATOR'S NOTE:

Father Yasuda does not address the question as to why identical wounds appeared on the *left* hand of Sister Agnes and on the *right* hand of the statue of Our Lady. Two questions are implied here: a) Why the wound? b) Why on the right and left hands of two persons, one in Heaven (Our Lady represented by the statue) and the other of a person here on earth?

As Father Yasuda explains, this type of miraculous wound is called a stigmata. It indicates the stigmatized person's participation in the redemptive suffering of Jesus. Over five hundred stigmatists have been recognized in the Church (although there have certainly been more.) And stigmata usually are recognized to be miraculous when there is not just the sign of a wound, but actual *bleeding* not caused by any natural means.

Bleeding from the hand of a wooden statue is obviously a miracle. And since it is miraculous, we are compelled to ask what Heaven is saying to us by causing the same wound to appear simultaneously on the right hand of the statue and on the left hand of Sister Agnes.

Among other meanings we can see here: a) The doctrine *"To Jesus Through Mary,"* taught by Saint Grignion de Montfort and recommended in the encyclical *Redemptoris Mater;* and b) The doctrine of co-redemption set forth in the same encyclical. Father Yasuda touches upon the latter but because of the importance of the miracle in the full context of the messages of Fatima and Akita, and especially in light of *Redemptoris Mater* (which appeared on March 25, 1987, after Father Yasuda's book was written) let us briefly examine these two teachings of the Magisterium in that important encyclical of the 1987-88 Marian Year.

To Jesus Through Mary

The first doctrine is that as Jesus came to the world a first time through Mary, so now He wills to come to the world again through Her but in an interior manner, making Himself one with us. St. Grignion says that TRUE devotion to Mary always focuses on Jesus while simultaneously recognizing the important role of Mary both in the Incarnation and Redemption. He says that Mary is by Grace what Jesus is by Nature and that we should lose ourselves completely in Mary's Immaculate Heart in order that we may more quickly and perfectly become one with the Sacred Heart of Jesus.

The blood flowing from the left hand of the sister and the right hand of Our Lady seems to symbolize the oneness of which Saint Grignion speaks: our oneness with Mary who is, in the order of Grace, really and truly our *Mother*.

But more important, as Father Yasuda stresses, is the message of *our calling to suffer with Mary* (as She suffered in all of Her sorrows and especially on Calvary) *for the salvation* of souls.

Co-Redeemers

We are all called to be co-redeemers with Jesus. And according to Saint Grignion de Montfort the most perfect way to respond is to unite ourselves to the most perfect of His co-redeemers, His own Mother... whom He gave to us from the cross to be also our Mother.

Saint Paul said (Colossians 1: 24) that by suffering he makes up for "what is lacking in the sufferings of Christ." This does not mean that there was something more that Jesus had to suffer, but that WE ARE CALLED TO SUFFER WITH HIM. We are called to help in the salvation of souls. We are called to be "co-redeemers." Monsignor Knox translates Col. 1: 24, "I am glad I help pay off the debt which the afflictions of Christ still leave to be paid for the sake of His Body, the Church."

As we shall see later in this book Our Lady has revealed at Akita that She has already been able to hold back a great chastisement of mankind by offering to the Father the Passion of Jesus, "His Precious Blood, and beloved souls who console Him forming a cohort of victim souls."

†††

Chapter Six

The Second Message of Mary

We recall that the wound first appeared on the hand of Sister Agnes on Thursday, June 28th. As we shall see, the miraculous events surrounding the great message of Our Lady to the world through Akita, were to continue with miraculous signs almost up to the time of the Bishop's pastoral letter of approval in 1984.

Then on Friday, July 27th, after reaching a peak of suffering, as announced by the angel the wound instantly and completely healed, leaving not a trace.

It is interesting that July 27th is the Feast of Saint Pantaleon, a martyr whose blood is said to liquefy each year on his Feast Day, as does the blood of Saint Januarius... a miraculous phenomenon repeatedly recognized by the Church and worthy of much greater meditation and attention.

On the evening of Saturday, July 28th, Sister Agnes was called to the Bishop's room. His Excellency asked her to recount what had happened the previous afternoon. She spoke of the voice of the angel which surprised her while she was praying in the chapel and of the intense pain which vanished as the angel announced. She spoke also, excusing herself for not having shown it to the Bishop, of the blood which appeared on the hand of the statue.

The Bishop listened with close attention as was his custom. He went back over the preceding facts, asking the same questions a little as one would review a lesson. He made written notes of each detail, perhaps to be sure that there was no contradiction. As for Sister Agnes, she invariably repeated over and over the same answers. As for the message of the Virgin, she hesitated a bit as to the way in which Our Lady had insisted that one add *truly* before *present in the Eucharist* in the prayer of the Handmaids of the Eucharist. (The Bishop had not taken any decision concerning this, using great prudence in everything.)

At the end he gave Sister Agnes an unexpected mission: "When this person returns, you will ask the three following questions:

1. Does Our Lord wish the existence of our institute?

2. Is its present form suitable?

3. Is a group of contemplatives necessary in a secular institute?"

This was not complicated and at the moment she agreed without difficulty. With time, however, she felt more and more the weight of this responsibility. The more she repeated the questions to herself, the better she understood their meaning. She said to herself that she would have to ask the questions with assurance. But in any event it was not she who would decide the moment... When would she be able to hear the voice again? And if this grace was not accorded to her...? Men can hope, but does not everything depend on the Will of God?

Totally powerless, her only recourse was to kneel often before the Blessed Sacrament to pray that the occasion might be given to accomplish the task given to her by the Bishop in the name of holy obedience.

August 3rd, 1973, First Friday

A week later Sister Agnes began her day with a longer period of prayer in the chapel than usual. The morning passed without any special event. However that afternoon, during her visit to the Blessed Sacrament:

"I remained to meditate on the Passion of Our Lord after 2:30 in the afternoon and I said the Rosary. Had perhaps an hour passed since I arrived in the chapel? That day the angel appeared (which had not happened for some time) and she recited the Rosary with me. During this time I had in my mind the questions of the Bishop and I secretly hoped that the occasion would present itself for me to ask them.

"Had the angel divined my desire? The occasion was quickly given: *'You have something to ask? Go ahead, you have no need to be troubled,'* she said with a smile, slightly inclining her head. Then taking my courage in two hands, very impressed, I was just saying the first word when suddenly from the statue of Mary, I heard as the first time that voice of indescribable beauty:

"'My daughter, my novice, do you love the Lord? If you love the Lord, listen to what I have to say to you.

"'It is very important. You will convey it to your superior.

"'Many men in this world afflict the Lord. I desire souls to console Him to soften the anger of the Heavenly Father. I wish, with my Son, for souls who will repair by their suffering and their poverty for the sinners and ingrates.

"'In order that the world might know His anger, the Heavenly Father is preparing to inflict a great chastisement on all mankind. With my Son I have intervened so many times to appease the wrath of the Father. I have prevented the coming of calamities by offering Him the sufferings of the Son on the Cross, His Precious Blood, and beloved souls who console Him forming a cohort of victim souls. Prayer, penance and courageous sacrifices can soften the Father's anger. I desire this also from your community... that it love poverty, that it sanctify itself and pray in reparation for the ingratitude and outrages of so many men. Recite the prayer of the Handmaids of the Eucharist with awareness of its meaning; put it into practice; offer in reparation (whatever God may send)* for sins. Let each one endeavor, according to capacity and position, to offer herself entirely to the Lord.

"'Even in a secular institute prayer is necessary. Already souls who wish to pray are on the way to being gathered together.** Without attaching too much attention to the form, be faithful and fervent in prayer to console the Master.'

"After a silence:

"'Is what you think in your heart true? Are you truly decided to become the rejected stone? My novice, you who wish to belong without reserve to the Lord, to become the spouse worthy of the Spouse make your vows knowing that you must be fastened to the Cross with three nails. These

---

*Words in parenthesis have been added by the translator.
**We might apply this to the prayer groups of the World Apostolate of Fatima (Blue Army cells), and similar prayer groups developing all over the world.

three nails are poverty, chastity and obedience. Of the three, obedience is the foundation. In total abandon, let yourself be led by your superior. He will know how to understand you and to direct you.'

TRANSLATOR'S NOTE:

This prophecy of a great chastisement was previously made at Fatima in 1917 in a series of prophecies, the last of which was: *"Several entire nations will be annihilated."* In March 1939, following the "great sign" which Our Lady announced at Fatima as a prelude to the Second World War, Our Lord told Sister Lucia (the survivor of the three children of Fatima):

"Ask, ask again insistently for the promulgation of reparation in honor of the Immaculate Heart of Mary on the First Saturdays. THE TIME IS COMING WHEN THE RIGOR OF MY JUSTICE WILL PUNISH THE CRIMES OF DIFFERENT NATIONS. SOME OF THEM WILL BE ANNIHILATED. IN THE END THE SEVERITY OF MY JUSTICE WILL FALL MOST SEVERELY ON THOSE WHO SEEK TO DESTROY MY REIGN IN SOULS."

Ten years before, Our Lady had asked for the collegial consecration of Russia to Her Immaculate Heart, promising that it would be a sign of Russia's conversion. But when the consecration was not made Our Lord said that it would eventually be accomplished, but: *"It will be too late; Russia will already have spread her errors throughout the world."* (Martin's edition of Lucia's Memoirs, Porto, 1973, Page 465.)

After the collegial consecration made by the Pope at Fatima on May 13, 1982, Lucia said: "The consecration will have its effect, but it is too late." She said that *to avoid atomic war now* (atomic bombs having proliferated to various nations) "The Blue Army (the World Apostolate of Fatima) *will have much to do."*

Sister Agnes now describes the effect of this major message at Akita on August 3, 1973.

"It was a voice of indescribable beauty such as there could be only in Heaven. I was far too impressed and overcome to wonder whether I was hearing with my deaf ears or with my heart. I was prostrate, unable to make the slightest movement. Even more, it was as if my whole body was alert not to lose a single one of the words.

"After the principal message, there was a pause. I do not know how to say how much time it lasted because I was completely absorbed in the present moment. Perhaps it was the space of an Our Father, perhaps too short to say even the first phrase. I think that I was no longer aware of time.

"I am asked also if I did not lift my head, because during the pause I might have thought that the message was over, but I could not because I was entirely under the influence of a mysterious force. To give a comparison, even when one knows that the song which one is listening to with delight is over when there is a pause, I felt clearly that it was not over. When the last word faded into silence, I knew it was the end as when a strong light is suddenly extinguished. Then I raised my face and saw that the angel had also disappeared.

"After the beautiful voice with the heavenly sound was quiet, I got up and remained a moment in prayer, so much did the sublime echo of that voice continue to resound within me. Then remembering that it was necessary to give a detailed report to Bishop Ito, I hastened back to my cell.

"Opening the notebook in which I registered all the events which had taken place for some time under the title of *Journal Of A Soul*, as the Bishop had requested I began to write. I wrote concentrating my thoughts and praying at each word, that each phrase be as exact as possible. The long message flowed from my pen without the slightest difficulty to my great amazement. I was able to put it all down straight away without the slightest hesitation and without the need of searching in my memory for the words which had become engraved in my soul and as though they were dictated by an invisible presence. I think this would have been impossible solely by my natural faculties.

"While writing, I experienced again the emotion felt at the very time of hearing Our Lady and at the same time I realized with gratitude and enthusiasm that the reply to the questions of Bishop Ito were contained in the totality of the message. Even when it came time for my profession on the 15th of August, I hardly had need to consult my notes, so easily did the words come back to me."

Before studying the meaning and the scope of this event, I would like to recall an anecdote which took place on this same evening of August the 3rd. In the middle of the night Sister Agnes was awakened with a start, *"Get up! Get up!"* She could not be mistaken. It was the voice of the guardian angel.

With a bound she was up and opened the door. A curious burning odor filled the corridor. Following the smell, she went down the stairs and hastened to the kitchen. The metal kettle on the stove was as red as a ball of fire! Now completely awake she had only time to turn off the gas. She got some water and threw it on the incandescent kettle. After a moment the steam began to dissipate and the kettle appeared, but in what a state! In the bottom, calcified leaves of herbs gave off a fetid odor. The next morning it was learned that a sister had gone to bed forgetting the kettle on the fire. A little while longer and the house might have been the prey of flames.

This was not to be the only happening of its kind for the community from this day. The guardian angel would more than once come to help in the daily things of the life in this community especially marked and chosen to be among the special souls whom Our Lady was now gathering together as those *"who will repair, by their suffering and their poverty, for the sinners and the ingrates."*

But now we know perhaps the most important part of the great message for the world which this community, and in particular Sister Agnes, had been prepared to receive. The second message of Mary contains major themes which form the central nucleus of Her words. It contains a teaching of the highest importance which is accentuated by the background of the miracle of the bleeding of the statue. The central theme begins with the words, *"Many men afflict the Lord,"* that is to say the sins which we commit daily in our earthly life. Mary searches the world with Her glance and seeks *"souls who console the Lord. To appease the wrath of the Father (She) awaits souls who repair, by their suffering and their poverty, for the sinners and the ingrates."*

The warning contained in the words, *"The Father is preparing to inflict a great punishment,"* is the consequence of what precedes. It is a pressing cry of distress leading to an explicit demand in the following sentence.

⌐ Here clearly appear the answer to the three questions of the Bishop. To the question, "Does the Lord wish the existence of our institute?" Mary answers with the simple words, "*I wish this also of your community.*" She thus recognizes the existence of the Handmaids of the Eucharist while at the same time making an appeal to all men.

To the second question, "Is its present form suitable?" She gives Her direction, "*Without paying too much attention to the form, be faithful and fervent in prayer to console the Master.*" She seems to wish to suggest that it is inappropriate to emphasize the distinction between a contemplative order, an active order and a secular order and that we should not put a scale of values among the religious belonging to different congregations. She thus reproves the attitude which looks to establish a hierarchy among the different categories of religious orders, a conception influenced by the spirit of the world which always seeks to make comparisons and segregations. She insists on the essential which is not the form but conformity to the will of God.

The third question finds an answer in the passage, "*Even in a secular institute, prayer is necessary... already souls who wish to pray are in the course of being assembled.*" Clearly whether a secular institute or not, even when one is in the lay state, prayer must be the center of life.

In the beginning, the Institute of the Handmaids of the Eucharist was a group of women living without a well-defined rule. The main principle was community life lived in simplicity and poverty by persons wishing to offer themselves in prayer.

Finally, when we look closely to the answers to the questions of the Bishop, given without awaiting the questions themselves, one is touched by the content and pertinence which could not be attributed to human wisdom, but which are indeed the very words of Heaven, of the Mother of God in person.

TRANSLATOR'S NOTE:

One might be surprised that Father Yasuda hardly comments on the terrible warning in Our Lady's message. He merely refers to this by remarking that it is in keeping with the miracle of the blood flowing from the statue which prepared Sister Agnes and the community for this somewhat frightful, even terrifying announcement from the Mother of God.

In his pastoral letter, Bishop Ito went so far as to say that if it were not for the miracles we might not be able to accept so grave a message.

However, this second message of Our Lady was not primarily to speak of the chastisement, but to speak of the need for souls gathering in prayer to make reparation in reply to the questions of the Bishop.

It is only about seven weeks later, on the 13th of October, that Our Lady will speak in detail about the chastisement which threatens the world if Her requests, first presented at Fatima in 1917, are not heard.

The Attacks of the Devil

We have already spoken of the helpful intervention of the guardian angel appearing to Sister Agnes. It is true that this kind of experience is rather rare and men today have a tendency to look upon it with a disdainful smile, and if they do deign to interest themselves in it, it is only to try to explain it away as a symptom of mental weakness.

However, as we have also remarked, the intervention of the angels was an important part of the events of Fatima and the important role of angels has been accentuated in a special way by the Church in recent times, especially by Pope John Paul II.

During the wave of criticism that followed the announcement of these events in Japan, one can imagine the reaction to which Sister Agnes was subjected from some quarters. But if she had much to suffer from bad spirits in a human sense, she had much more to suffer from the fallen angels for whom hell was created.

We can pass over the threat of fire on the very night after the message of Our Lady, but the following day, the 4th of August, as Sister Agnes was about to go into the chapel for the evening office, she felt herself brutally seized by the shoulder and drawn backwards. Because of the violence of the gesture, she understood at once that it was not simply someone accosting her. In her surprise she turned to her left and what she saw was like a dark shadow leaning over and dominating her entire height. Frightened, she lifted her hand to free her shoulder, but the grip that held her as though in a vice prevented any movement. With a shiver of fear she implored, "Hail Mary! Guardian angel, save me!"

Immediately the angel appeared and advanced her into the chapel. The force which held her shoulder prisoner immediately left. She could finally wet her finger with holy water, make the Sign of the Cross, and take her usual place with the community. Even though it lasted but a short time, this unusual attack, sufficient to cause nightmares, is certainly beyond the domain of human capacity.

Later the same incident took place at the same spot. Immediately she begged, "Lord, save me, have pity!" and was immediately freed. She understood at once that these attacks came from the devil. And while the meeting of divine grace fills the heart with sweetness and interior peace, this kind of experience leaves a sinister aftertaste and a sensation of fear.

For Sister Agnes, it was her first experience of this kind since her arrival at the Hill, but not the first in her life. She recounts a similar memory which even today causes a cold sweat when she thinks back upon it:

"It was when I was convalescing in the hospital in Myoko. I think it was the 20th of January. My condition had improved and as I had been advised to take a thermal treatment I went to the bath every morning after my temperature was measured. That day I went with another invalid of advanced age. When we entered the baths they seemed deserted. I had hardly begun to disrobe in the women's vestiary when I saw Mr. T.

"Mr. T. was an invalid gravely ill. He had been a practicing Catholic but one good day one no longer saw him in church. Some very believing persons who saw that his end was coming were concerned about his soul, and they exhorted him to become converted but without result. He no longer wanted to hear speak of religion. These persons had asked me to go to see him in his room because among invalids there was a kind of bond. I did this more than once. In the beginning he was hard, but little by little he loosened up and even accepted that I give him a prayer book and a Rosary.

"At the time that I was in the thermal bath I had understood that he had gone back to his family for a rest cure. While I saw him standing before me I was dumb-founded. He had an anxious, tormented air with deep wrinkles between his eyebrows. I could not keep from speaking to him: 'But Mr. T., what are you doing? You are in the woman's section here!'

"Then a black shadow which was leaning over him from the back began to suddenly grow. Then it unclenched its long, repulsive and grasping fingers with which it had gripped his shoulders, deployed black wings like those of a great bat and cast itself on me... What happened then? When I saw its fingers like grappling irons precipitating upon me to snatch me, I was so afraid that I fainted. I learned later that the companion who was with me pre-vented my falling and hitting my head on the concrete floor. I was taken immediately to the hospital where I remained ten days unconscious.

"My body was rigid as a corpse and everyone thought that this time it was the end. On the third day they gave me the last sacraments. The doctors were saying that if I did survive there was a fear of cerebral lesions or blindness. When my mother saw my eyes covered with the white membrane, she would have preferred that her poor daugh-ter, who had already seen so much in life, be not made to suffer more.

"Despite my comatose state, I am told that I had the peaceful expression of a child and, strangely enough, when one called me I answered with a voice of a child of five or six years and made childish responses, 'I'm going home, I'm going home' and when one asked me why, I replied, 'To play with papa and mama, to play ball.' My mother was saying that if the good God would take me in this state of candor I would surely go to paradise.

"As for me evidently I had not the slightest idea of what was happening around me. All that I remember is that I saw myself seated, overcome with fatigue, after having walked in immense fields which extended beyond my view. But there were beautiful flowers there and I was not at all bored.

"Then the sisters of Notre Dame of Junshin of Nagasaki (to whom I belonged at that time) sent me some Lourdes water. Hardly had I been given a swallow than my hands and feet, as stiff as wood, began to move. And as though I were coming out of a long sleep I stretched out, extended my hands into the air and exclaimed, 'Oh, how beautiful.' I did not know that the flowers I had seen in the fields during my 'sleep' were those at my bedside. Then my strength returned and I was completely better.

"The digression is a little long but it must be added that two months after my cure the wife of Mr. T. came to see me: '... Before his death my husband told me how grateful he was to you for having saved him by your prayers,' she said, thanking me. But when I told her of the frightening meeting in the bath she stated, to our great surprise, *that had been the very moment when Mr. T. received the last sacraments.*"

This true life experience shows well how the devil hates in particular those who do good, especially when they snatch souls from him. In the lives of the saints one finds numerous examples in which he shows his hatred in one form or another seeking to place obstacles in the way and to avenge himself.

It is also important to note that Sister Agnes was not at all instructed in the things of the devil. She knew that he existed. That is an article of faith. But she had no idea as to why she was the object of such attacks. Moreover, Satan's methods went far beyond anything she could have imagined. Characteristic in this regard is the example of the Cure of Ars, whose feast is on August 4th (the day Sister Agnes was first seized by the shoulders as she was entering the chapel where Our Lady appeared to her) who even gave the demon a nickname.

It is a recognized fact that the holy Cure of Ars was assaulted many times by the demon under visible and invisible forms because he snatched so many souls from him. The saint never let himself be battered down and when he saw his room burned he said with an understanding smile, "It's the Creeper again..." and added, "Unable to catch the bird, he burns the cage."

Certain paintings represent the devil as a monster with the wings of a bat and fingernails or grasping fingers like grappling hooks. Sister Agnes had never seen such paintings nor had she ever read the life of the Cure of Ars.

It would seem that this experience was given to her in order that she might feel the need of seeking the aid of the Lord, of His Mother, and of the angels in all circumstances, and remain vigilant in prayer.

Light, Perspiration and Perfume

Almost two months later, on the 29th of September, all the community had gone into the city to attend Mass in the parish church for the feast of Saint Michael. When they came back, following the meal, Sister Agnes and a companion went into the chapel to pray the Rosary.

At the beginning of the fifth decade Sister Agnes saw that the statue of Mary shone with a brilliant light. She tugged at the sleeve of her companion. Both saw the light shining from the statue as they continued to pray. It was the garment which shone the most, but also from the two hands there emanated a dazzling light.

The fifth decade completed, they approached. While Sister Agnes prostrated herself, her companion pointed her finger towards the hand, "Oh! The wound has disappeared!"

As we remarked before, the blood had flowed for the last time on the 27th of July, but the trace of the wound was always on the hand of the statue, even though it had disappeared from the hand of Sister Agnes that same day.

Now also on the statue it was as though there had been nothing there. They stood astonished, seeing the state of the hand suddenly become intact as it had been three months before. They decided not to speak of it to the others before informing the Bishop.

However, during the course of the evening office an unusual event occurred which brought the metamorphosis of the statue to the knowledge of all. As the office was almost over, the statue again became resplendent in light and began streaming as though with perspiration.

Sister Agnes who had her head lowered suddenly felt someone beside her. She lifted her eyes and saw the angel who said: *"Mary is even sadder than when She shed blood. Dry the perspiration."*

She joined the other sisters who brought a sack of cotton. Five of the sisters, with great care and devotion, sponged the perspiration. The entire body was soaked. They had to dry and dry; a liquid similar to heavy sweat oozed without stopping, especially on the forehead and the neck. In addition to the general amazement there was a shared feeling of grief. Sister K. prayed with tears in her voice, "Holy Mary, pardon us for causing you so much sadness and pain. We beg you pardon for our sins and our faults. Protect us, help us!" Each sister applied herself to drying the area before her eyes with the same common intention of reparation and veneration. The pieces of cotton were wringing wet.

After dinner the community returned to see the statue. It was again wet with perspiration. Distracted, the sisters began again to dry it. One even heard Sister O., not naturally talkative, murmur in a sad voice, "My cotton does not absorb. One would say that there is no perspiration when I dry." Immediately, as if in answer to her anguished words, the cotton that she was holding began to absorb the perspiration like a sponge plunged into water... which impressed her very much.

Suddenly one of the sisters remarked that the cottons had a fragrant odor. Each one began to smell the cotton she was holding and they discovered a subtle fragrance which they could not describe as rose, violet, or lily. There was general delight. One had never experienced such a marvelous fragrance. And when Sister O. declared that not even the most subtle of perfumes give off such a sweet fragrance, it was indeed the opinion of everyone. They were asking if this might not be the perfume of paradise.

The following Sunday when they entered the chapel they were struck with the same perfume. The superioress went to see whether the fragrance was coming from the statue while the others, remaining in place, felt enveloped in its delicious waves. The grief of the previous evening caused by the discovery of the perspiration gave way to peace and joy which shone on all the faces.

This fragrance remained for a long time in the chapel. Each time one entered, one had the impression of being transported into Heaven.

October 7th, the Feast of the Holy Rosary

Sister Agnes applied herself to saying each bead of the Rosary with particular attention. And the hearts of all the community seemed in the maternal embrace of Mary and lifted up in a spontaneous transport to the Lord. Sister Agnes felt so happy that she asked herself how long this might last, "If that could continue for the whole month of the Rosary!" And immediately the angel appeared at her right and lightly shaking her head said with a smile:

"Only until the 15th. After which you will no longer be able to experience this fragrance on the earth. You also amass merits, as so many delicate perfumes. In bending all your efforts to this, under the protection of Mary, you will succeed." Saying this she disappeared.

As the angel predicted, the perfume remained until the 15th of October. It was especially strong on the 3rd, Feast of St. Therese of Lisieux, and on the 15th which was the last day. For all the sisters this grace was a great consolation. They saw in it an encouragement to support all the difficulties which would present themselves in the days to come.

Although Sister Agnes has played a key role in all of these events, it was obviously now a *community* matter. Had not Our Lady said that each member of the community was dear to Her, and that She was gathering together souls who would pray, make reparation, and console the Lord?

From now on, all the community will be ever more deeply involved both in the wonders that are to follow and in the trials to be endured. Now all the sisters had seen the light shining from the statue. As all of them had experienced the sense of grief because of the blood flowing from a wound in Our Lady's hand, so now also they said they felt a sense of grief as they each participated in drying a miraculous perspiration which emanated from the statue in such quantity that it soaked the cotton they used to dry it.

It is proper to reflect on this new metamorphosis of the statue of Our Lady on the Feast of Saint Michael, who is venerated as the holy patron of Japan. The trace of the wound on the hand, which had been there for three months, disappeared at the moment when the statue shone forth with a dazzling light.

That evening *all the sisters were eyewitnesses* of the real prodigy of the wound disappearing, and of the perspiration. And when the cotton was sent to the official laboratory of the University of Akita the scientists found, as we shall explain later, that it was human! *These were visible (and now scientific proofs) that what was happening here was truly from Heaven.*

Further was the fact that the cotton impregnated with perspiration from the statue itself exhaled a subtle and unknown perfume, an unquestionable supernatural sign.

I myself arrived at Yuzawadai six months after this event. When the sisters spoke to me about it, in the beginning I did not know what to think. I didn't see the need of verifying the truths of the facts because I was sure that a judgment would be rendered in good time on the entire matter.

One day when I was receiving a visitor, one of the sisters brought one of the pieces of cotton so that he could smell the perfume. When I saw his reaction, I smelled it in turn (I was not very sure of my ability in this regard because I had undergone an operation on my nose in my childhood). It was true. To my surprise it gave off an ineffably subtle fragrance not even equaled by a rose. My hesitations and doubts suddenly fell away and I had the immediate feeling that this was a question of an important event.

So I can imagine the impact it must have had on each of the sisters when they actually dried the statue, and then experienced this wonder. Like Saint Thomas, do we not all have a tendency not to believe what we do not see, what we do not touch with our fingers, what we do not verify with our senses?

From that moment I have been led progressively to be the witness of the mysterious phenomena of which I write.

The Guardian Angels

I would like to go back here to something which happened a few days before. It was the 2nd of October, Feast of the Holy Guardian Angels. One can easily understand the joy and thanksgiving of Sister Agnes on that day, she who had communicated with her guardian angel "in person." From the time that she no longer could hear, how many times had the angel not appeared to extend a helping hand? She had even given Sister Agnes counsel, encouragement and assurance of her protection. She must have been so happy to be able to assist at the Mass celebrated by the Bishop, to pray and to thank her guardian angel for so many graces received in this very chapel.

Sister Agnes recounts what she experienced during the Mass: "It was during the Mass at 6:30 in the morning, at the moment of Consecration. A dazzling light suddenly shone forth. It was the same as I had seen during three days beginning on the 12th of June and which had so much overwhelmed me. I had the feeling that this adorable splendor was that of the presence of Our Lord Jesus Christ in the Eucharist. Struck to the heart I could only repeat, 'My Lord and My God!'

"At the same moment there appeared the outline of angels in prayer before the shining Host. They were kneeling all around the altar in a semi-circle, their backs toward us. There were eight of them. Evidently they were not human beings and when I say kneeling, that doesn't mean to say that I saw their legs or how they really were. It is difficult precisely to describe their clothing. All that one can say is that they seemed to be enveloped in a sort of white light. Certainly they resembled human beings, but they did not have the air either of children or adults, how to say... finally, beings to whom one could not give the age. This said, one could see also that they were not the fruit of an optical illusion and that they were truly there. They did not have wings, but their bodies were enveloped in sort of a mysterious luminescence which clearly distinguished them from humans.

"Amazed, not believing my eyes, I opened and closed them, rubbed them, but nothing changed. All eight were there to adore the Most Blessed Sacrament in an attitude of great devotion.

"Before so strange a sight, either I was too moved, or even overcome by the brilliance of the light. I thought of nothing else and forgot to respond to the prayers. Since the chapel is quite small, and I was in the front row, a little to the left of the altar, I found myself completely absorbed by this luminous scene which unfolded before my eyes. Not that my movements were not in accord with the others who rose and knelt, but quite simply I believe that I thought of nothing else.

"At the moment of Communion, my guardian angel approached me to invite me to advance to the altar. At that moment, I clearly distinguished the guardian angels of each member of the community close to their left shoulders, and of the height a little smaller than each. Like my guardian angel they gave truly the impression of guiding and watching over them with sweetness and affection. This scene in itself opened my eyes to the profound meaning of the guardian angel, better than had any theological explanation, even the most detailed. After dinner I gave the complete account of this vision to the Bishop.

"There were indeed eight angels there at the moment, while we were seven. With the Bishop it made eight... Had they not chosen the Feast of the Guardian Angels to show the example of adoration and to reveal their readiness to lead us to the Lord?"

Bishop Ito at the Akita Convent.

Chapter Seven

The Third Message of the Virgin

It was Saturday, the 13th of October, the anniversary day of the great miracle of Fatima, a miracle witnessed by about one hundred thousand people and performed by Our Lady at that predicted time and place "so that all may believe."

This morning as usual Lauds were followed by a time of adoration. Reciting the Rosary, Sister Agnes again saw the luminous splendor of the Blessed Sacrament. From the tabernacle the brilliant light seemed to spread into the whole chapel. At the same moment the statue of Mary gave off a celestial fragrance which filled the chapel. Ravished, Sister Agnes forgot the passage of time and had to leave the holy place with regret when it came time for breakfast.

Then she went to her room but she was still too distracted to give serious attention to her work. Shortly afterwards, her companions turned over to her the care of the house while they left for the city. She profited from this to go back to the chapel where she decided to say the Rosary.

She relates: "Taking up my Rosary I knelt down and made the Sign of the Cross. Hardly had I finished when that Voice of indescribable beauty came from the statue to my deaf ears. From the first word I prostrated myself to the ground concentrating all my attention:

"'My dear daughter, listen well to what I have to say to you. You will inform your superior.'

"After a short silence:

"'As I told you, if men do not repent and better themselves, the Father will inflict a terrible punishment on all humanity. It will be a punishment greater than the deluge, such as one will never have seen before. Fire will fall from the sky and will wipe out a great part of humanity, the good as well as the bad,* sparing neither priests nor faithful. The survivors

---

*For suggested explanation of these mysterious words see the booklet *The Meaning of Akita.*

will find themselves so desolate that they will envy the dead. The only arms which will remain for you will be the Rosary and the Sign* left by My Son. Each day recite the prayers of the Rosary. With the Rosary, pray for the Pope, the bishops and the priests.

"'The work of the devil will infiltrate even into the Church in such a way that one will see cardinals opposing cardinals, bishops against other bishops. The priests who venerate Me will be scorned and opposed by their confreres... churches and altars sacked; the Church will be full of those who accept compromises and the demon will press many priests and consecrated souls to leave the service of the Lord.

"'The demon will be especially implacable against souls consecrated to God. The thought of the loss of so many souls is the cause of My sadness. If sins increase in number and gravity, there will be no longer pardon for them.*

"'With courage, speak to your superior. He will know how to encourage each one of you to pray and to accomplish works of reparation.'

"When the Voice was quiet, I gathered the courage to raise my head and I saw the statue still brilliant in light, but a slight expression of sadness seemed to veil Her face. Then I resolved to ask the question, 'Who is my superior?' And at once I felt a reproach from the angel who had appeared at my side during the interval (I did not hear this reproach in a living voice I simply felt her say to me, 'On such an occasion you would certainly have been able to ask something more important.' But as I had three superiors in addition to the Bishop I had thought it opportune to ask it.

"The Voice at once replied:

"'It is Bishop Ito, who directs your community.' And She smiled and then said: "'You have still something to ask? Today is the last time that I will speak to you in living voice. From now on you will obey the one sent to you** and your superior. Pray very much the prayers of the Rosary. I alone am able still to save you from the calamities which approach. Those who place their confidence in me will be saved.'"

---

*For suggested explanation of these mysterious words see the booklet *The Meaning of Akita*.
**This is Father Yasuda, author of this book. (*Translator*)

"She had finished speaking. This time my lips were numb with emotion and I was able only to say 'yes' while I bowed to the ground. Little afterwards I lifted my head. The dazzling light had disappeared and there remained only the wooden statue which had resumed its normal state and stood there, silent, in its humble and poor corner of the chapel.

"The light had disappeared, but the Voice remained engraved in the depths of my soul and I was filled with fear and thanksgiving at the idea that a person like me had been able to have the grace to receive messages of such importance. I prostrated myself to the ground again knowing only to repeat:

"'Holy Mary, refuge of all sinners, pray for us.'"

Now we know the great message for which there had been such a long and painful preparation! The messages were given on three separate occasions through the intermediary of the statue. And *even as at Fatima the six apparitions of Our Lady terminated on the 13th of October, so on this 13th of October Mary gave Her last message at Akita.*

It is unthinkable that this could have been by chance. Everyone knows that there is a "third secret" of Fatima which was communicated to Pope John XXIII, the Holy Father in 1960. At the time the Pope decided that it should remain a secret.

When this message was published in Japan some critics, who claimed that this was all out of the mind of Sister Agnes, said that she was probably inspired by reports of what the third secret of Fatima contained.

It seems that any doubts of Bishop Ito concerning this were dissipated after numerous interviews with Sister Agnes during which he was able to question her in detail. He knew her well as her spiritual director and certainly his detailed questioning was to avoid any possible misunderstanding. Furthermore, the first time she communicated the third message she did not know the meaning of the word "cardinal," because the Voice had employed the English word "cardinal" pronounced in Japanese. The Bishop was very impressed when she asked, "What does that mean, 'cardinal?'"

"But it is the English word for *sukikyo* (Cardinal in Japanese)," he answered.

"Ah good! Then that was it?" She had finally understood. "Yes, *sukikyo*, I learned that word in my catechism, but 'cardinal' I had never heard and I was asking what that could be."

This simple detail shows beyond doubt that Sister Agnes was completely incapable of having invented the text of the messages. Ten long years after this event, it is no longer possible to nourish the slightest doubt on this subject.

If then the third message of Akita has been judged credible, one can imagine to a certain degree what must be the content of the third secret of Fatima. On October 13th at Fatima 1917, following the great miracle which was witnessed by thousands over an area of 32 miles "so that all may believe," the primary message to the world was, *"Men must stop offending God Who is already so much offended!"*

And the heart of the third message given by Our Lady at Akita is a warning which can be summed up thus, *"If men do not repent and better themselves, there will be a terrible chastisement."* At Fatima Our Lady had said that if Her requests were not heard "error will spread from an atheist Russia throughout the entire world, fomenting further wars, the good will be persecuted, the Holy Father will suffer much, *and several entire nations will be annihilated."*

Sister Agnes said that after Our Lady spoke the face of the statue had an air of sadness. Has not Our Lady permitted us to see Her profound maternal concern, concerning how many of Her children will indeed mend their lives by prayer and acts of adoration? Despite the great miracle at Fatima, recognized so signally by the Church and by two personal visits there by popes, there has not been an adequate response.

Our Lady repeats the same warning in this locality of Akita, Japan, by the intermediary of a modest statue of wood and a humble nun, leaving the seal of the supernatural by indubitable wonders.

From all of this, there comes forth an awareness of something serious, grave, solemn, pressing each and every one of us to realize his and her personal responsibility.

Perfume and Stench,
October 15th,
Feast of Saint Teresa

As the angel had predicted (on October 7th, the Feast of
Our Lady of the Most Holy Rosary) October 15th (Feast of
St. Teresa of Avila) was the last day of that wonderful
perfume of Heaven. Indeed from the morning onward
it impregnated everything with a special intensity and
filled the sisters with complete delight. In contact with
this subtle fragrance which no earthly rose could equal,
one can only say over and over that it was the perfume of
heavenly flowers, so marvelous that one would never
forget it.

The next day, October 16th, what the sisters encountered in the chapel had nothing whatever in common with
what they had experienced the day before: *an indescribable
stench.* Nor was this stench ordinary. Like the perfume
which had no equivalent in anyone's memory, this terrible
odor was strange. It didn't seem to resemble any other
smell and seemed to come from another world. *And there
was something else,* as Sister Agnes relates:

✔"The odor which assailed me when I opened the door of
the chapel was so disagreeable that I had the reflex action
of placing my hand on my nose. As the sacristy seemed to
smell more than the rest, I told myself that perhaps the odor
was coming from there and I went looking for some infected
place but found none. Furthermore, it was not the odor of
a dead animal. Others thought at once that it might be
coming from the compost pile, but that was at the other
extremity of the building. In any event, it was time for
Lauds and we were forced to pray while repressing our
disgust.

"Then, after the Rosary, Sister K. got up to extinguish the
candles burning in front of the statue. Suddenly she
jumped, pointing her finger at the front of the knees of the
sister next to her. The latter lowered her eyes and saw
something like a grain of white rice which she took into her
fingers, 'Bah! A worm!' I heard her cry. At the same time,
each one saw that there was a worm in front of the sister

next to her, 'Look! There too!' each one remarked in turn with a shiver of disgust. They looked in every possible corner from which the worms might have come, but they encountered nothing but the mysterious stench and it was impossible to determine the origin.

"These two events did not fail to liven the conversation during the meal. They felt it so much the more because of the marvelous perfume which had delighted them for 17 days and all agreed by saying that this stench too was not a natural phenomenon, but something which came from the occult world.

"When I saw that white and slimy worm, I could not help but think that the image of my repulsive state was reflected to me. And the others seemed to feel the same. After an almost euphoric period when we had been bathed in celestial waves for more than two weeks, this was the cold shower making us quite small. The beautiful fragrance was the perfume of Mary, free of all stain of sin. The bad odor was of us, covered with sins. When the first disappeared, it is we who gave off the odor. What are we then when the grace of God is withdrawn? Are we more than one of those miserable worms? Each one took this reflection personally.

"The worms appeared only once, but the fetid odor remained for three days."

The Fourth of November

On November 4th the Bishop came, and as usual, he asked if there was anything new. Sister Agnes told him of what had happened beginning with the message of October 13th.

The following morning while Sister Agnes assisted at the Mass celebrated by the Bishop, the angel appeared after Communion: "Your superior is getting ready to request from Rome the official recognition of your institute which he had desired for a long time. Announce that there will be many obstacles, but it will please the Holy Father to grant it because Mary has encouraged him to love poverty and to accomplish acts of reparation."

These words were conveyed to the Bishop immediately after Mass.

A little after the New Year, on the 30th of January, another unusual event occurred. There was an unusual snow fall that year, beyond what anyone had ever seen in that region. It was the heaviest snowfall recorded since the creation of the weather station of Akita, and January the 30th was especially memorable in this regard.

That night Sister Agnes woke up three times. The first was a little after midnight, then at one-thirty, and again at twenty minutes to four. Each time she woke from the same dream: The roof of the house was on the point of collapsing under the weight of the snow and she felt herself trying to hold it up with both her arms, exhausting all her strength. In her dream when her arms began to fail, Sister Agnes' guardian angel appeared and came to her relief. Indeed, she had come to help three times. When Sister Agnes awoke she had a stiffness in her shoulders, was gasping for breath, and her body was bathed in perspiration.

She had to reassure herself that it was only a dream, but just the same she was nevertheless concerned at seeing the snow continue to fall without letup. At the rate at which the snow was falling, the house would certainly be very heavily covered and there was good reason to fear that the roof would give in under the mass of snow. The following morning it would be necessary to arrange for the removal of the snow as soon as possible... She awaited the dawn with concern.

When she woke up at 4:30 it was still dark outside but one could see, through the falling snow, a pile of at least six feet of snow on the roof of the priest's house opposite the convent. Sister Agnes wanted to do something but unable to undertake such a heavy work, she hardly dared to present this problem before the others.

After Lauds, taking advantage of the breakfast time, Sister Agnes made her concern known to the person responsible and begged her as soon as possible to do what was necessary. But she was not taken seriously. The beams were sufficiently strong and they would not budge under a little snow! Then Sister Agnes recalled a frightening memory that she had of the house which had collapsed under snow when she was in Myoko. But the responsible person was not convinced. Still filled with concern, Sister

Agnes decided to ask one of the other sisters to intervene, hoping that she would be more convincing. This time the person responsible decided at least to go and see. What she saw caused her to turn pale.

Already a large part of the roof had sagged to within less than a foot of the window frames. But by a miracle, it remained at a normal height above the room of Sister Agnes and thus formed a sort of square hat falling side to side of the window. Before this sight, which spoke for itself, the person responsible was most impressed. "It is indeed the protection of Heaven which has avoided a catastrophe! This is something truly remarkable!" The alarm was given. There was panic. Something had to be done, and quickly! In the village everyone was taken up with the same problem but finally two men of goodwill were found who climbed to the roof and caused a veritable curtain of snow to fall.

Sister Agnes looked at the white sky which continued ceaselessly to discharge its overload and she imagined with a shiver of fright what would have happened if no one had noticed. She thanked Divine Providence for having spared them a catastrophe, the consequences of which one can only imagine. She still felt the effects of the combat that she had endured in her dream. Her arms were stiff and her legs so weak it was as though she had come to the end of her strength after climbing a high mountain. She had difficulty breathing and although she had always shown a resistance to every trial, she asked the superioress for permission to take a little rest in the afternoon.

At the end of the snow, when one came to repair the roof, the carpenter could not hide his amazement; 42 beams had broken. Needless to say, the news was the occasion of renewed acts of thanksgiving!

If these above events are not directly connected with the statue of Our Lady and Her message, they were nonetheless lived by the entire community.

The first was the insupportable stench which infected the chapel for three days after 17 days passed in the atmosphere of Heavenly perfume. And while the latter came from the statue, one could not determine the origin of the other. They looked at every nook and cranny, thinking it might come from the body of a dead cat or mouse, but nothing was found. And as for the worms which so unexpectedly appeared in front of each of the sisters, efforts to find the source were also fruitless.

If the fetid odor evokes something occult and not from this world, the worms seemed also to have a symbolic meaning. Furthermore, the place most infected by the stench, where it was truly unbearable, was the sacristy *which also served as confessional.* The opinion spread through the community that it was "our sin." As Sister K. said, "The sweet perfume is the odor of the Blessed Virgin; this stench, comes from us. While the grace of the perfume plunged us into joy, the latter brought us face to face with our reality." And this reflects the opinion of the entire community. As for the worms which suddenly appeared under their noses, they strongly report the feeling, "What am I compared to God? I am but a miserable worm!"

Aside, it is interesting to note that in the beginning no one remarked that the worm was in front of herself, but noticed first of all the worm in front of the sister next to her. "One never takes account oneself of his pitiable state," they remarked and their comment is quite pertinent.

Worms appear often in sacred scripture as the symbol of the soil and bitterness brought on by sin. Our Lord Himself describes the frightful state of desolation into which fall the souls that go to hell, "Where the worm never dies and the fire is never extinguished."

This world in which we live could also indeed become a place fragrant with benedictions and divine grace rather than an infamous cesspool worthy of the malediction and anathema of the Most High. In the first case, it is like a garden in which men travel toward life eternal under the impulse of grace; in the second, man is separated from God, at the edge of a precipice over a world of hatred and despair.

Without ambiguity, these facts show the choice which is left to our liberty, like signs at a crossroad. And they are all the more meaningful and deserving of our reflection in that they follow so closely upon the communication of the third message.

The second event concerns the catastrophe avoided thanks to the "combat" by Sister Agnes with the help of her guardian angel. That the community had been protected by means of her feeble body has also a symbolic meaning: Those who respect the message of Our Lady and put it into practice are assured of the protection of Heaven, which also implies the supernatural aid of one's guardian angel.

Christians today, including the Catholics influenced by modern society, have a tendency to give value to an abusive scientism which minimizes the action of the supernatural. The value of the latter is indeed recognized in the sacraments, but outside it is overlooked. Contemporary man seems to have a repulsion for everything that touches upon the intervention of angels in our human society. He has a marked taste for psychology applied to just about everything, thinking in this way to explain supernatural phenomena and to deny in particular the existence of angels (both the fallen ones who would drag us to hell, and the guardians who would guide and protect us).

In the present case, one can clearly see the link of solidarity which exists between the supernatural world and our physical world. Is not this event a supplementary proof for the action of the angels as efficacious intermediaries between the celestial universe and the physical universe?

The mystery of the Incarnation of the Word in the womb of the Virgin Mary began with the oral announcement of the Angel Gabriel. It was through the intermediary of an angel that union between God of the Holy Trinity and the human person of Mary took effect. There is nothing surprising about an angel intervening still today in our daily life as mediator of the Divine Will. And still more, this shows to what point God surrounds every creature with His loving regard.

Thus this event, which might not seem of great importance, *can help us better understand the message of Mary which is aimed at drawing us from sin and enabling us to turn back a chastisement worse than the deluge.*

Love of the Neighbor

On Monday, February 25th, the guardian angel appeared during the evening Rosary at the beginning of the third decade. She murmured to Sister Agnes: *"At this moment one of the sisters is tormented by something. Take from her an object she wears and wear it in her place until the First Friday of the month. On that day, I will give you the answer she needs."* Then the angel disappeared.

Discreetly, Sister Agnes went to the kitchen and approached the sister who was taking care of the stove and without giving much thought as to what she should choose, she noticed the medal which her friend was wearing around the neck. She undid the chain saying, "Lend it to me for a little and I will explain to you afterwards." Sister Agnes put the medal around her own neck and returned to the saying of the Rosary. It all happened so quickly that she herself was surprised.

However, something even more surprising then followed. When she tried to take up the prayer, she found that her mind was elsewhere and that she was incapable of doing it. She had to reason with herself that "You are before the Lord, you must pray with all your heart..." but she could no longer concentrate at all. Her thought was scattered. Her heart was filled with ideas without relation which came and went like clouds in the sky... For the first time in her life she understood the meaning of "not being able to pray."

Her companion had spoken to her before of difficulties that she experienced because of distractions, but she did not understand it and always asked the reason. "What does it mean to be distracted?" Sister Agnes had asked of the others. She finally understood that it was not given to everyone to be able to be completely absorbed in prayer, each one being more or less subject to caprices of thought. She had been careful not to insist, in order not to give the impression that she seemed to have received an exceptional grace.

However, she had indeed received this rare privilege, namely the faculty of praying in a spirit of total abandonment and total simplicity of heart. From her infancy she had shown a special aptitude for concentration. She absorbed herself totally in what she undertook. This natural disposition made it possible for her to enter without difficulty into a life of prayer when she embraced the Catholic faith. When one asks her how she prays her answer is of a disconcerting naivete. She explains that she quite simply follows the counsel of the priest who prepared her for Baptism: to pray is to speak with God and nothing more. When one asks her if she is not troubled that the One to whom she is speaking does not answer, she said that that is no problem because anyway, she was always the dear child of her father, and consequently she speaks to God as if speaking to her father. For Mary it is the same: she speaks to Her in the same way as to her mother. Such are her answers, given with a disarming naturalness.

Does not the evangelical recommendation "like little children" refer to this fundamental attitude of the heart? And when one tries to know if other thoughts do not come to trouble her prayer, Sister Agnes answers with a troubled air, "How can one think of anything else when one is before God and speaking to Him?"

Thus in prayer said aloud, it is enough to think of the sense of each word. Finally she sees before her the faces of all the people whom she carries in her intentions, with just enough time to stop on each one in particular. So how would she have time to think of anything else! Furthermore, Sister Agnes seems to believe that this is evident for everyone.

Thus this new experience astonishes her so much the more because she had not the slightest idea of the difficulties one can experience in prayer. Suddenly her thoughts begin to wander from right to left and everything around her begins to bother her. Until then expressions which express embarrassment and affectation such as "to put on airs," to "show off," were for her only words. For the first time in her life she understands what they mean in reality.

Now she realized what it was to be in this insipid and heavy state. Moved by a profound compassion, she nevertheless forced herself to pray that her companion might be liberated. During this time, her companion from the kitchen shone with a radiant enthusiasm. Never in her life had she succeeded in praying so easily.

Two days after this began was Ash Wednesday, the 27th of February, a day of fast and abstinence. Sister Agnes knew through the Gospels that prayer and fasting were efficacious to dissipate this kind of torment. On that day, she deprived herself more than the others to obtain the requested grace. Giving the impression that it was because of the state of her stomach, she did not take a drop of water the whole day. She repeated without stopping, unable to do more because of the state in which she found herself, "Lord have pity!" and begged Mary without being able to find words other than, "Help me!"

That evening the Way of the Cross began at 7:30. She followed this sorrowful spiritual exercise to the end doing violence to her somber and recalcitrant humor. But hardly was the service over than she felt in herself a ray of light piercing through the darkness. Somewhere a flame had been lit and comforted her with its warmth. As though returned to herself, she found that she had regained her habitual disposition. The following morning she welcomed the day with the same interior peace.

For her part, her companion from the kitchen seemed closed within herself and spoke to no one to such a point that she finished by going into her room for the rest of the day. Now Sister Agnes knew what it was to have such a suffering, having had the same experience. She went often to console and encourage her friend with the words of one who had known the same lot: "We will offer all our weaknesses and our miseries to Mary and ask Her help." She continued discreetly, to the degree that was possible, to fast and to pray.

The First Friday of the month of March came, day of the angel's promise. That morning her friend hastened to greet her and with a radiant face exclaimed: "Thank you for your prayers!" She confided to her to have really felt the effects, but nonetheless Sister Agnes did not relax in her effort.

That evening when the two sisters were alone in the chapel after the Way of the Cross, the guardian angel appeared to Sister Agnes and gave her this exhortation which she felt was addressed to her friend: "Believe, trust, pray!" She repeated it to her friend word for word. "I believe, I trust, I pray," * repeated the other. Then the angel

---

*This is similar to the prayer taught by the angel to the children of Fatima: "My God, I believe, I adore, I trust, and I love Thee! I beg pardon for those who do not believe, do not adore, do not trust and do not love Thee!"

disappeared. Immediately Sister Agnes noticed that she was holding in her hand the medal she had borrowed, and gave it back. The latter put it around her neck and went and knelt before the statue of Our Lady saying aloud, *"Holy Mary, I believe, I trust, I pray!"*

If this religious had not been delivered immediately from the cross which she had been given to carry, she had received the confidence and the hope of being able one day to overcome her trial.

This episode, which ought not to surprise us, concerns the interior world in its most pure expression. At first sight one would be tempted to see simply a beautiful story between two friends, one of whom frees the other from a burden by sharing her sufferings through prayer and fast.

Indeed this experience was as fruitful for Sister Agnes herself. These three words faith, hope and love give her the measure of the trials which are going to mark her road and they create in her the necessary dispositions to overcome them.

The current fashion, spread even among religious, tends to consider all that carries the name of God as an object of intellectual investigation and not as a Being to Whom one gives confidence. In the Catholic Church one hears again and again that theological matters are evaluated and researched with intellectual delight. However, when one stops at believing only what one has understood at the end of a research, can one speak of a deepening of the faith? Has one not merely rested on the level of acquisitions of human intelligence?

No matter what one does, human resources alone are always powerless to sound the immeasurable depths of the Divine mystery. The only way to progress at all is to have recourse to the grace of faith which is a gift of God. One often hears it said: Without previous knowledge, one cannot pray to God or confide to His Providence. This is to rely on one's own ideas and to count only on one's own strength. It is hardly possible in these conditions to have a taste for prayer to Him who is radically different, God in His ineffable mystery.

The world we see is full of marvels which far surpass our human capacity of knowledge and comprehension. As for the spiritual world which we do not see, the feeble light of our intelligence is of little help. It is only by the light of faith that we can hope to penetrate in some small way the depths of the Infinite Mystery. For those who put intellectual knowledge above all, the tribulations of a soul in search of God taken upon herself by a compassionate sister will appear like something of little consequence. But it is a profound act of charity.

The effective participation of Sister Agnes in the moral sufferings of her friend, on the invitation of the angel, is a very concrete example of love for one's neighbor. In our days this kind of love is hardly taken into consideration. But it is necessary to remember that the saints who have marked the history of the Church were men and women who never recoiled before suffering out of love for their neighbor. Inversely, when one is consecrated only to preaching while remaining in delicate comfort, one has little chance of seeing that preaching bear fruit.

What the angel teaches us through this experience of Sister Agnes is certainly not visible to the eyes. It is nonetheless an exemplary application of the command-ment of Jesus. Today, love for one's neighbor has a tendency of being considered only as a material act consisting of giving and receiving to the degree that one's pocketbook does not suffer too much. Is this sufficient indeed to please the Lord? The teaching of Christ is not easy: "What merit have you for loving those who love you? When you salute only your brothers, where is your merit?"

In this trial the exhortation of the angel to believe, confide, and pray, is a precious encouragement for Sister Agnes herself more than for anyone else in the numerous difficulties she was soon going to have to face when the message of Our Lady would be made public. She was to be submitted to test after test, repeated interrogations, disbe-lief, and worse. In all this the encouragement of the angel to "believe, trust, and pray" will be a consolation. All her trials to this date were preparing her *to bear a much greater burden.*

All of the events that I have recorded up to this time had taken place in the year which preceded my arrival, beginning in January, 1973, when Sister Agnes was struck with total deafness. Not having been a personal witness during those previous years, I have had to rely on the intimate journal of Sister Agnes, filled out and explained in detail in my direct communications with her and with the members of the community. Now I, too, became a witness.

The 10th of March, 1974

It was on the 10th of March, 1974, when I decided to take a leave of absence from public preaching and to take up residence in the presbytery of the sisters of Yuzawadai, at that time a hamlet unknown to the world and buried under snow. I have already told you of the unusual circumstances which led me to this isolated convent and made me, however unworthy, a part of the extraordinary events which surround the presentation to the world of a message of stunning importance.

What I learned and what I personally witnessed concerning the statue of Our Lady and Her message to the world, was completely beyond anything I had foreseen. From this point forward I will be recounting the facts as I personally lived and observed them.

In my younger years I wanted to be a priest because I wished to preach the Word of God. And having realized my wish by the grace of God, I thought only of consecrating the rest of my days to this task without ever in the world thinking that I would come to dwell in this convent lost in the northwest mountains of Japan.

It is always with emotion that I recall the unusual circumstances of Divine Providence which led me to this place... an invisible thread of Providence drawing me through the Immaculate Heart of Mary.

TRANSLATOR'S NOTE:

It was proposed to Bishop Ito that the first major book in English about Akita should be based on the writings of Father Yasuda (that is, this present book), on the book by Father Shimura (who was Vice Rector of the cathedral in Tokyo and spiritual director of the Blue Army there), and in a special way on the intimate relationship between the events and message of Akita and the events and messages of Fatima. However, Bishop Ito directed that first of all this book of Father Yasuda should be translated and made available in English in its entirety. And this is because it seems apparent that Our Lady Herself prepared and chose this exceptional priest to go to the convent at Yuzawadai at precisely the time he did so that he could closely study the event as the confessor and spiritual director of the community, become the confidant of Sister Agnes and the right hand of the Bishop in evaluating and reacting to this most important supernatural intervention, so important not only to Japan but to the entire world.

As remarked in a previous footnote, rarely has any important private revelation been the object of such prudent, discreet, and accurate "immediate" reporting. One can recall the role of Blessed Claude de la Colombiere in the apparitions of the Sacred Heart to Saint Margaret Mary, the records of Our Lady of Pontmain by Abbe Richard, or the role of Canon Formigao in the apparitions of Fatima. None exceed in importance the role of Father Yasuda in the events of Akita. He now continues.

Sister Agnes greets a group of U. S. Pilgrims.

Chapter Eight

Days of Hesitation

When I arrived at the hamlet of Yuzawadai, which was just coming out of its winter hibernation, I first had to adapt to the rhythm of the simple life of the convent.

The sisters did not delay in recounting to me the events which had happened during the previous two years, happy finally to find someone in whom they could confide. At the beginning I was completely abashed. One cannot immediately believe this kind of thing. Furthermore, the principal witness of the events, Sister Agnes, had nothing in particular which distinguished her from the others. She appeared to me as one of the most ordinary of women. What I heard seemed to be something of a dream, or of a world disconnected from reality. I had no idea from which angle to approach it.

When one starts to tell you about angels here and angels there, anyone would have difficulty in knowing how to answer. And then is there not the world of the apocalypse in which the angels fly in the air at their will without bothering anyone? But I have now come to understand that it is impossible to understand anything at all of the events described up to this point if one did not first of all recognize the reality of the angel which appeared to Sister Agnes.

In my life, I had never heard spoken about angelic apparitions, either near or far, except through the accounts of the Bible. Even guardian angels... did they show themselves so easily as this? For my part of course I believed in their existence, but it was something which remained purely in the domain of faith. Also, when I was told that the angel of Sister Agnes appeared to her and spoke to her and replied to her like a human person, I was perplexed. Even if this truly happened, I felt the need of tangible proof.

That is why, without categorically denying what I had heard, I was hoping within myself for a sign worthy of faith to bring light on this enigma. Although I think I had the best intentions in the world, I felt the need of discerning whether these manifestations were real or an hallucination coming from the profound depths of the human psyche.

But never for a single instant did I think that the person involved was schizophrenic. Gradually as the days passed, it became more and more evident that she was not different from any of the others. This is especially true about her attitude during prayer which showed no anomaly, and also her faith in general which never gave the impression of being especially privileged. She was in every way similar to the other religious. Even during the conversations at table she was talkative like the others and even had something of a tenderness in her manner even if she should speak emphatically, or when she made a mistake on the meaning of certain words. (We must remember that she participated in a conversation only by lip reading.)

A month and a half passed in this state of doubt, questioning, waiting for "something which would permit me to believe."

The Japanese Garden

It was after mid-April before spring began to warm our frigid regions of the north and the last snows were disappearing in the hollows of the valleys, giving way to the scintillating flight of the day flies. As I gazed at the beautiful country around me, from the fields that surround the convent to Mount Taihei which rises in the distance above the neighboring hills, my heart stirred within me with the thought of a new project.

The Japanese countryside is very much appreciated because of its variety of form, mountains, rivers, and the richness of its phases in the four seasons, and in the midst of the most beautiful parts of the country one is almost certain to find a religious monument constructed in some past epoch. This was impressed upon me each time that I visited such sites, beginning with Mount Koya, Mount Hiei, or temples like those of Eiheiji. It seems to me that the same is true in Europe where the major places of pilgrimage are often situated in a natural setting suitable to meditation.

Long before I came to Yuzawadai I had desired to do something to encourage the cult of the Virgin Mary in the heart of the Japanese. When I thought of the deep roots which Christianity implanted in countries of Christian tradition, often the fruit of great sacrifice, it occurred to me that these roots had to be nourished by more than just ancestral tradition or the acceptance of a dogma in the strict sense of the word. The lives of numerous saints suffice to show that there is something more... a simple and fervent devotion to the Virgin Mary.

It is certainly a unique benefit of devotion to Mary that the Christians of Europe have been able to cultivate and conserve their Christian faith intact after more than two thousand years. Closer to us is the fact that the "hidden Christians" of feudal Japan were able to keep their faith in Christ despite terrible persecutions, sustained by the devotion to "Santa Maria" to a point that fills us with admiration.

Based on these thoughts, I came to ask myself if the protection of Mary and authentic Marian devotion would not be a precious help to contribute to the work of the Christianization of Japan. For this reason I had had a statue of Our Lady of Lourdes made for the church of which I had charge before I came to Yuzawadai on the occasion of the centenary of the apparitions. I had it placed in the church garden, wanting to transform the same garden into a Japanese Garden of the traditional style. The atmosphere of the Japanese Gardens is especially adapted to recollection. I had begun the project. But a great deal of money is necessary to complete a project of this scope and I was unable to obtain the support of the parishioners at the beginning. I decided to start, confiding the enterprise to the protection of Mary, and indeed my confidence was recompensed beyond all hope. I thank Heaven and continue to pray for all those persons who contributed to that work.

So the project which began to form in my mind at Akita, as I contemplated the beautiful countryside there, was far from a caprice.

This had nothing to do with what the sisters had been telling me. I was still in the state of perplexed waiting described above. *I was not yet sure that Mary was truly present in this place in a special way.* But if it should prove to be true, the arrangement of a "Garden of Mary" where one could pray would certainly be a precious help in the future. So I proposed the garden to the sisters of the community to see what their reaction might be. They all agreed with common accord, assuring me of their full cooperation. Obviously there was at once the eternal problem of finding the funds. One can imagine the cost involved in landscaping about six and a half thousand square meters!

The superiors of the convent took advantage of a visit to the Bishop who was hospitalized at that time to ask if he would be favorable to such a project. As could be expected, the Bishop was reticent since there was no evident source of funds. They told the Bishop that they had no idea yet of a budget but at least they could begin and leave the rest to Providence. It was the thread in the needle. The Bishop finally gave his consent. And the news that the Bishop had given his "official authorization" filled the community with joy and hope. It even seemed to increase the community courage in the fulfillment of daily tasks.

The project of "The Garden of Mary" was each day a part of the intentions of the community prayers, always asking the special intercession of Saint Joseph.

On May 1st, Feast of Saint Joseph the Worker, conscious of the financial burden implied by such an enterprise, I said some words at the beginning of the Mass in honor of Saint Joseph: "Today we honor Saint Joseph, patron of workers. We ask his very special intercession for the realization of the Garden. Since Saint Joseph passed his life in the service of the Lord and of Mary in self-abnegation, we are sure that in Heaven he will aid us with the same joy to bring this project dedicated to Mary to fulfillment. We celebrate the Mass for this intention."

After breakfast which followed the Mass there was the usual time of adoration. Then Sister Agnes approached me and said: "The guardian angel who often gives me precious counsels appeared during the adoration and said: 'The intention which you offer in conformity with the will of him who directs you is good and pleasing to the Lord and His Holy Mother. The more you offer this good intention, the more difficult and numerous will be the obstacles.

"'But today you have asked the protection of Saint Joseph in a same union of prayer. This prayer is very pleasing to

Jesus and Mary; it will be heard. Saint Joseph will protect your work. To overcome the exterior obstacles, pray with confidence in interior unity.

"*It is rather a shame that there is no exterior sign here in honor of Saint Joseph. Ask him who directs you to do this when you can, even if it is not right away.*'" Having said this the angel disappeared.

(After this a statue of Saint Joseph was placed in the chapel. The present statue was offered by a kind person some years later. It was made, like the statue of the Virgin, by Mr. Wakasa who sculptured it from the same kind of wood as the statue of Our Lady, so that it is complementary.)

This was the first time in my life that directly from the mouth of Sister Agnes I heard speak of the special intervention of a guardian angel. However, the truth of the prophecy depended obviously upon the real success of the enterprise which remained to be verified. But the following ten years progressively opened my eyes to the reality of the events.

TRANSLATOR'S NOTE:

In his modesty, Father Yasuda does not draw our attention to a most important fact in this very first message of the angel bearing directly upon himself. We will recall that in the very important message from Our Lady, She Herself spoke of the superior and also of *the director sent* to Sister Agnes, *in whom she was to confide.* And now the guardian angel confirmed specifically that this director is Father Yasuda... "the one who directs you."

We remember that it was in that all important third message of October 13th, just five months before Father Yasuda came to Yuzawa-dai, that Our Lady said to Sister Agnes: "Do you have something more to ask? Today is the last time that I will speak to you by voice. From now on you will obey *the one who is sent to you* and your superior."

A Garden Consecrated to Mary

The idea of arranging a Japanese-style garden in honor of Mary in a remote corner of our country did not long

remain just an unacted upon pious wish. The announcement of the angel that *"The intention which you offer...
pleases the Lord and His Holy Mother"* encouraged us to
undertake the work without delay despite any obstacles.
For someone whose reason for living is the service of the
Lord, the difficulties encountered become a part of the
program.

I recall the encyclical of Paul VI *Marialis Cultus*. In that
long encyclical addressed to all the bishops of the world on
the Feast of the Presentation of Jesus in the Temple, the
Holy Father meditated on devotion to the Virgin Mary
concluding with these words: "If I have considered it
necessary to speak at such length of cult and devotion to
the Mother of God, it is because it is an integral element
which cannot be separated from our Christian faith. Also
the importance of the problem required it." And in the first
part of the encyclical the Holy Father underlines that, "True
growth in Christian faith is always accomplished by a just
and balanced progress in piety towards Mary."

It was a reading of these words of the Holy Father in the
encyclical *Marialis Cultus* after my arrival on the hill of
Yuzawadai which revived in me the desire of a greater
intimacy with our Holy Mother.

In my young years, it was after having heard a sermon
about Mary that I made the decision to consecrate my life
to the priesthood. During my years of preaching I often
exhorted the faithful to a greater filial love towards Mary,
trying always myself to remain faithful to the daily recitation of the Rosary which I advised. It was because of this
that more than once it was said behind my back that I was
that "backward Marianist."

Today, following the so-called renewal of the liturgy, one
sees the statue of the Virgin less and less in churches, and
especially in modern churches. It often happens that She
is also taken out of all churches or that a much smaller
statue is used, or even relegated to the entrance as a sort
of decoration. When one hears this expression "backward
fanatic" in this context, one asks oneself how those who use
it would interpret the words of Paul VI in the encyclical
Marialis Cultus: "The cult owed to the Mother of God is an
indissoluble element of our Christian faith.

During the time that I had charge of a parish, I dedicated an important part of my pastoral work to this problem. It was the time when the National Union of Youth had taken the lead in a general agitation throughout the country, the repercussions of which were felt even in the Church through the action of progressive priests. To preach Marian devotion in such an atmosphere was chancy, but I never abandoned the struggle. This true battle, drawn up in the bosom of the Church, will long remain engraved in my memory.

When I think back on this, I recall a scene of the Way of the Cross represented on a picture which I used to have. As Our Lord advances carrying His cross, before and behind Him children, unaware of what they do, brandish signs upon which are inscribed the crimes and the punishment to be inflicted upon the Condemned while others pull upon the ropes which hold Him. And Christians today who give so little importance to the Mother of Jesus appear like these turbulent groups. Oh, what a sad spectacle for those who consider Her as truly their own Mother!

The new sects which rise up today in Japan, without speaking of those which existed from previous times, are never stingy about the acquisition of lands and materials necessary for their cults. But is it not curious that the religious and the Catholic lay people of our country, who confess faith in the one true God, Creator of all things, show a bewildering indifference when it comes to these exterior manifestations? When they acquire property they use it to construct secular structures. I recently saw a grotto of Lourdes transformed into a parking lot. Was that not appropriating purely and simply something which had been consecrated to the Lord?

One often hears the progressives, consecrated or lay, remark that it is no longer necessary to construct churches. It suffices to say Mass in the homes of the faithful. To live the word of God is above all to participate in social life. To serve one's neighbor is more important than to assist at Mass. And it seems that these opinions are taken as authentic by not a negligible number of Christians. One shouts that this is an involved way of "living Christ."

Such persons forget that God is the Unique Source of authentic love for one's neighbor. Such a love is not possible unless it is lived in the spirit of offering to Him Who gives it. Christians must be aware that love of one's neighbor without reference to God is a tree, stripped from its roots.

Today it is popular to speak of "innovation" on all levels; one speaks frequently of "revolution," of "newness," to bring in things often doubtful. The religious renewal is in itself most praiseworthy, but if abuses come to wipe out its sacred character, one must fear that the life of faith will sooner or later be deprived of vital nourishment. This danger requires from the faithful the greatest vigilance. When the statue of Our Lady wept for the first time at Yuzawadai on the 4th of January, 1975 (an event which we will describe in detail shortly) the angel told Sister Agnes:

"The Holy Virgin... loves Japan. She has therefore chosen this land of Akita to communicate Her messages... She awaits you with open arms to pour forth graces. Spread devotion to the Virgin."

From Plan to Realization

Although the miracle of the tears had not yet taken place in confirmation of the messages given by Our Lady through the statue of Akita (this was to happen only seven months later) the project began to take shape on the first of May, 1974. It was still too early to go immediately ahead. But I decided, with the agreement of the community, officially to inaugurate the works with a ceremony on the 31st of May, Feast of the Visitation of Our Lady.

Indeed the previous day had been marked by an unusual event. All had decided to go to the chapel and I was also there when one of the sisters turned suddenly and announced in a sharp voice, "The face of Mary has changed!" Immediately raising my eyes I saw that the face no longer had the same color; it was of a dark reddish brown, distinctly different from the color of the rest of the statue.

Feeling the excitement gathering around me, I kept my usual attitude while letting them know that this was now a moment to pray in silence. After the office, the sisters discussed among themselves what they had felt in seeing the new expression of the statue. (It was an event experienced by the entire community.)

Sister Agnes later told me what she remembered of that moment: "When I had dried the perspiration which came from the statue, or when I had seen the wound on the hand I was shocked. How is that possible? Simply a wooden statue! But this time I felt very strongly that the statue of Mary was alive!

"While the garment and the hair retained their look of natural wood, the face, hands and feet alone became distinguished by a dark reddish-brown tint such as skin bronzed by the sun. It was not a dark, more or less dirty color. It was a beautiful reddish brown, lustrous and touched with life. Ah, it was indeed a living Mother! I still recall the joy I felt at that moment!"

Apart from the hands, the traces of this change are still visible even though the color has since diminished. Eight years later when the sculptor came to see the statue he could not hide his amazement. It can happen that entire parts of sculptured wood change color, but it is unthinkable, by natural laws, that certain very determined areas become distinguished from the others by taking on a particular tint. He also showed himself intrigued by the expression on the face which had changed since the time he had made the statue.

I know that I am getting slightly ahead of the sequence of events, but I cannot help but remark that from that time many who came to venerate the statue said that it seemed to take on a different expression at different times. Another prodigy is in different expressions, sometimes striking, which appear in the various photographs. A question I often asked myself was not so much about the change of expression but why had the color changed? I seem to find the answer in a message given by Mary to Don Gobbi of the Marian Movement of Priests which I read quite a few years later:

"*The signs which I accomplish through the intermediary of My statues or My images are given to awaken in you a just devotion which give so much joy to My heart... these signs of My face... the face which changes color... these signs of My heart... My heart which sometimes exhales a discreet perfume and at other times an essence more intense.*

"When a mother experiences great joy her face blushes, and when she is worried about the future of her children she blanches. What is true of mothers on earth is also true of Me. If I give such signs so human and so maternal it is to show you that I am with you at each moment of your existence..."

In the same message to Don Gobbi, a little further one reads: *"The perfume which I exhale, sometimes intense and at other times subtle, is a sign given to show you that I am always with you and in particular at the moments when you need Me most."*

For the ceremony of the inauguration of the work, we invited persons from the village, especially those who had helped in the clearing of the land for the convent of Yuzawadai when the first members of the community came there: the Bonzess of the neighboring temple, friends from the parish of Akita and other regions, members from nearby branches of the Institute of the Handmaids of the Eucharist, and nearby relatives. Some had come from a distance to give their support. All in all there were about 30 persons. The little ceremony took place around a provisional altar erected for the occasion in the general area where there would soon rise a statue of the Holy Virgin in the center of the proposed garden.

In my introduction, I explained that this Japanese Garden in honor of the Virgin Mary was destined to receive persons who wished to pray, not only from Japan, but from the extremities of the earth. Afterwards I said the prayer of blessing and turned up the first shovel of earth. Those present took the shovel one after the other to complete a hole in the bottom of which we buried a Miraculous Medal from the Rue du Bac (convent in Paris where Our Lady appeared in 1830).

The second step now was to gather stones of different sizes for the arrangement of the garden. With the community car, we made several return trips all the way to Mount Taihei, along the river banks, and from the side of Oga, to gather stones which we piled into boxes. During this time we made the acquaintance of Mr. N., a solid and jolly man who helped us to transport more than two hundred stones from the River Kosa at the foot of Mount Chokai. And the sisters had not abandoned us. There are two memorable episodes.

One day the wheel of the car transporting the stones came off and rolled into the ravine, so heavy was the load. The stronger helpers hastened to lend a hand while others went to the chapel to say a Rosary. Shortly a bulldozer passing by solved the problem. Also, Mr. N. came in the fall with a bulldozer and began the important work of leveling the entire area.

Naturally everything stopped during the winter, during which we regathered our strength! When the first melting of the snows came, the work began again, and I joined the farmers of the neighborhood who came to help us, exposing myself with them to the snow and the rain, to the winds and to the sun, working the shovel and pushing the wheelbarrow.

Active participation in these physical works taught me much about the meaning of work. Is not the expiation of our sins by Jesus who carried the cross on His shoulders the heaviest of physical labors? This reflection permits me now to recognize a precious stone in each drop of sweat shed in the course of our work. Meditation on the Word is important, but accompanied by physical labors and moral pain, does it not lead to a more vivid experience of a love of Christ and a more intimate union with Him? At least such is the grace that I felt in making my humble contribution to the arrangement of the Garden of Mary.

The work was going well when, towards the beginning of July, the sister in charge of the funds gave us news which had the effect of a cold shower: "My Father, when we will have paid those who are working now, there will remain nothing more in the account."

I asked all to pray very much to Saint Joseph. For my part, taking advantage of the Feast of Obon, the 15th of August, (a Buddhist Feast) I decided to give the workers a vacation during the month of August. The end of that month brought us a great surprise; a check of several million yen was sent to us by a sympathetic person who regretted not being able to participate personally in the work. From this time on we were able to continue the work without interruption. One could cite example after example of intervention which truly came from Heaven. It was towards the end of May or the beginning of June, during the third year of the work, that we received a rather disagreeable visit. It was the time of the commission inquiry on the events concerning the statue which had been formed at the request of Bishop Ito. And since we are speaking here of the Garden, it seems the appropriate place to mention how even this came under adversity in this trying moment.

At the time, I was away giving a talk which had been requested from outside. A person who claimed to be an important member of the Canonical Commission of Inquiry and authorized by the Bishop to take over spiritual direction of the community, announced to the latter: "The phenomena which occurred in connection with the statue of Mary are not a supernatural grace. They are only the result of ectoplasmic faculties of Sister Agnes and one must not use them to take advantage of people. The arrangement of the Garden of Mary is an act of propaganda which can only lead people into error and you must stop it immediately..."

It was only a week after my return that the sisters, not a little put out, told me about this. And I at once remembered the word of the guardian angel, *The more you will offer this good intention, the more numerous will be the difficulties and obstacles.* For my part I do not remember ever for one moment having conceived the project of the Garden of Mary with relation to the events connected with the statue. As I stated earlier I had accomplished a similar project, on a small scale, in the parish I had served before coming here. My sole desire was to create a propitious space for prayer, where one could be recollected in a calm atmosphere. Independent of the reality of the mysterious events of Akita, the idea of the Japanese Garden was unrelated. Over and beyond this kind of malevolent criticism I was resolved to carry on the work, cost what it might. But obviously there came dark moments when I came close to the point of letting everything go.

By October of this same year, thanks to the precious help of numerous well-wishers, the Garden of Mary was almost finished. The ceremony of the inauguration took place on October 11th, in the presence of the mayor of Akita and of numerous personalities and well-wishers who came from far and near. For this beautiful Feast, more than two hundred were present.

I presented the Garden of Mary with these words: "The principle part of the Garden is the pool in the form of the Japanese archipelago, from the middle of which rises the statue of Mary. In the background, water cascades from an artificial hill symbolizing the grace of salvation spread upon humanity, the source of which is the Cross of Christ raised on Mount Calvary. The ensemble therefore represents the water symbol which spreads over Japan through the intermediary of Mary, Mediatrix of all Grace. The little grass covered hill situated in the center of the Garden symbolizes peace and harmony by its round form, and recalls at the same time the Sermon on the Mount. The two extremities of the pool are separated from the central part by two bridges, Japanese style, leaving the Isle of Kyushu to the south and the Isle of Hokkaido to the north, with the flow of water... which represents the Jordan... oriented from south to north.

"The main entrance gate is made of two trunks of special wild trees of Akita, about two hundred years old, bearing up a roof of tiles which appear also to be old. Indeed it was conceived to give the Garden the majestic and sacred character evoked by its very name: *Gate of Heaven.*

"One can progress around the central little hill and the pond, visible from every part of the Garden, while reciting the Rosary. Furthermore, the entire layout was planned in order that one may always see Mount Taihei, and no trees were planted to risk losing the view of its changing and varied tints in the course of the year. More than a hundred different trees have been planted. Ninety percent of them have already taken root. And we can imagine how great will be the beauty of these plantings, brought from all regions of Japan in testimony of affection for Mary, in the years to come... "

The help which we received during these three years came to us from all the regions of Japan: from the island of Kyushu to the isle of Hokkaido for the glory of the "Celestial

Mother" and was literally providential. Now that it is finished we can indeed understand the prediction of the angel: *"The difficulties and the obstacles will be numerous,"* and her exhortation, *"Pray with confidence with interior unity."*

And all these things helped to prepare us for what was still to come!

†††

Above: U.S. Pilgrimage in the garden of Akita standing before a copy of the Akita statue. In his address to the pilgrims, Bishop Ito said: "The message of Akita is the message of Fatima."

Chapter Nine

The Healing Announced by the Angel

Now let us return to Sister Agnes, beginning in the month of May when we started the work on the Garden. What had struck me in reading the notes and messages of Sister Agnes was the prodigy that she was able to hear the words of the angel and of Our Lady even though medical science had declared her to be completely deaf. In the final analysis, this could only have been by "interior locutions" which have nothing to do with the physical faculty of hearing. Sister herself explains: "It was not the sound of an ordinary voice which would have resounded in my ears as if they had been temporarily healed. It was a voice which came directly to my heart, passing through my ears which were incapable of hearing."

In the first message of Our Lady, they were words of encouragement: "*Is your deafness difficult to bear? You will soon be healed, be sure. Be patient.*" In view of this prophecy, I said to myself that the extraordinary phenomena of the statue could never be recognized until the ears of the sister would be completely cured. Furthermore, I felt that the only way to prove the supernatural origin of Our Lady's messages would be a healing obtained not by medical treatment, but by the action of a supernatural force. Clearly, *a miracle was necessary.*

For my part I had no difficulty believing that sooner or later the healing would take place as the Blessed Virgin had predicted. When I finished reading the notes, I gave them back to Sister Agnes with this counsel: "Certainly one day you will hear again. But since the Lord loves sacrifice, abandon yourself entirely to His Will, without being concerned about being cured or not being cured, in a spirit of patience."

I knew very well what this must have cost her and I knew from the expression on her face as she read my lips that she had indeed resolved to give herself totally to the Will of the Lord.

Eighteenth of May, 1974

On May 18th, after the morning Eucharistic adoration Sister Agnes came to see me and said: "Just now, shortly after the Rosary and during the prayer silence, the guardian angel came to me and said: *Your ears will be opened in August or in October. You will hear, you will be healed. But that will last for only a moment because the Lord still wishes this offering and you will become deaf again. In seeing that your ears are restored again, the heart of those who still doubt will melt and they will believe. Have confidence and pray with good intention. Report what I have told you to him who directs you. But speak of it to no one else until it takes place.'"*

Later, in the notebook where these words were copied she adds: "In the beginning the angel was smiling but then her expression became severe. Already I did not believe my eyes, but when I saw her severe air, I felt my body contract under the surprise and I prostrated myself. My heart was full of an overwhelming joy mixed with the feeling that I had to be totally abandoned to God's Will. I said an ardent prayer of thanksgiving for so much mercy.

"When I told this event to the Father, he appeared very interested. 'Ah good,' he said. 'In August or October?' he repeated with a nodding of the head."

Indeed, what I was thinking was that if it was in the month of August it would certainly be the 15th, the Feast of the Assumption or on another Marian Feast Day, although the month of the Rosary might be more appropriate... My imagination was going!

After this Sister Agnes had to bear an unexpected trial which affected her in body and spirit as though in preparation for the graces she was soon to receive.

It was the morning of Thursday, August 8th; during the Mass I was suddenly seized with terrible stomach pains and had to be taken in haste to the hospital. I at once underwent surgery and if my days were not counted, I was immobilized in the hospital until the 4th of September. On my hospital bed I said to myself that the cure of Sister Agnes would perhaps not take place during this period. After I came out, when I had just about regained my usual schedule, Sister Agnes came to tell me on the morning of the 21st of September after the adoration: "A little after the beginning of the silent meditation the angel appeared and said: *'You spoke this morning at table concerning the dream, didn't you? Do not be disturbed. Today or tomorrow begin a novena, one of your choice, and then two more. During the time of these three novenas made before the Lord Truly Present in the Eucharist, your ears will be opened during the adoration and you will hear. The first thing that you will hear will be the chant of the Ave Maria which you are accustomed to singing. Then you will hear t he sound of the bell ringing for the Benediction of the Most Blessed Sacrament.*

'After the Benediction you will calmly ask the one who directs you to have a Canticle of Thanksgiving sung. Then it will be known that your ears hear again. At that moment your body also will be healed and the Lord will be glorified.

'When he learns this, your Superior will be filled with courage, his heart will be consoled and he will bear witness. However, the more you offer with good intention, the more there will be difficulties and obstacles. To overcome these exterior obstacles, pray with more confidence in interior unity. You will be protected, be sure.'

"After a silence, the angel added: *'Your ears will hear only for a certain time. They will not yet be totally cured. You will become deaf again. The Lord still wishes this offering... Report what I have told you to him who directs you.'* After having fixed upon me her profound regard, she disappeared from my eyes."

On these conditions, since the angel made everything so clear, I counseled Sister Agnes to begin the novena without delay, even the same day if possible, reminding her not to speak of it to anyone. Concerning the dream of which the angel spoke (*You have spoken of the dream this morning at table*) we will explain later.

Once again I asked myself when the grace of the predicted healing would be granted. If Sister was going to hear the chant of the Ave Maria and the sound of the bell, it would be during Benediction of the Blessed Sacrament, and that would surely be on a Sunday. And as the angel said that it would be during the time of three novenas

I made the mistake of thinking that it would be at the end of the third, that is the last Sunday of October. Even with predictions so clear, our intelligence slips into erroneous conjectures. It goes without saying that the human mind is truly not so smart.

Thirteenth of October, 1974

October 13th of 1974, anniversary of the third message of Our Lady here in Akita and also anniversary of the great miracle of Fatima, was a radiantly beautiful day. I took advantage of a few hours to go as far as Tenno, situated at the top of the Oga peninsula, carrying with me my fishing gear. As I had adoration of the Blessed Sacrament at 5 o'clock in the afternoon, I intended to return to compose myself a little before going to the chapel.

That evening exposing the Blessed Sacrament and incensing the altar a thought crossed my mind: *Could this not be the day?* After the Act of Contrition I returned to my place and joined in the Rosary. Then came the chant of the Ave Maria... it was towards the end of the chant, Sister Agnes prostrated herself on the floor and I saw that she was weeping. After the silent meditation and the usual prayers of Lauds came the moment of the blessing with the Holy Eucharist. One heard the sharp tingle of the bell rung by one of the sisters. Raising the monstrance I traced the Sign of the Cross, praying, "Lord, give Your grace according to Your Will!"

Then kneeling before the Blessed Sacrament exposed I began the divine praises, "Blessed be God... " At the end as I was getting ready to indicate a hymn, Sister Agnes, to whom I had turned my back, spoke, "My Father, may we sing the Te Deum, hymn #12!"

I immediately turned around and said, "Do you hear again?"

"Yes, I have just received this grace," she answered, without need of having to read my lips.

Therefore, I told the congregation (on Sunday there were also people from outside who assist at the ceremonies): "Today as the angel had predicted two times, in May and in September, the ears of Sister Agnes have been restored to hearing; this has just happened. In thanksgiving let us sing the Te Deum."

The news seemed to have produced a strong impression on those present who were unable to believe their ears... the proper expression here!... and some sobs mixed with the singing in an atmosphere charged with emotion.

Sister Agnes herself recounts what happened when she was cured: "At the moment of Benediction of the Blessed Sacrament, as the angel had indicated before, I first heard the voices singing the Ave Maria as though in the distance, as though in a dream. I heard only the voices and nothing else. Then there were some moments of silent meditation followed by the usual evening prayers, but of those I heard absolutely nothing. At the very instant when Father gave the Benediction of the Blessed Sacrament, I clearly heard the sound of the bell. Then I heard him begin, 'Blessed be God.' It was the first time I was hearing his voice.

"In the beginning when I heard the singing of the Ave Maria, an immense feeling of gratitude and of confusion filled my heart at the thought that God had leaned down to so small a thing as I. I was so overcome that I prostrated myself weeping. Finally able to stifle my voice, I no longer even found words for prayer.

"During the year and seven months that I had been plunged into a world of total silence, my parents were desolate and it was for me a nervous tension renewed with each day. And even now that my hearing was restored, I knew that a day would come when I would have to offer the privation of hearing once again and I fortified myself saying that it was necessary to continue to pray with more faith.

"The announcement of the angel, '*At that moment your body will also be healed,*' also had its effect. I noticed that the intestinal and other pains which had tormented me at this time had disappeared at the same moment."

Immediately, a telephone call was made to the Bishop to give him the news. Sister Agnes herself, with transports of joy, told His Excellency everything and answered his questions. She was also able to telephone her parents and close relatives to tell them of her unbelievable cure. At the request of the Bishop, I accompanied her to the hospital of the Red Cross and to the Municipal Hospital of Akita to undergo medical examination. Both establishments certified that her ears were now normal.

Two weeks later I was invited to speak in the church of Sister Agnes' native village to which I had accompanied her with two other members of the community. Her family, who had awaited her impatiently, assailed her with questions to see if truly she heard. It was a moving scene even for persons outside the family.

She did not forget the provisional nature of her state telling herself each day that it might be for only a week, or nine days, or forty days. She thanked Heaven for the unexpected grace of being still with normal hearing almost six months later. It was about the time of Ash Wednesday, in February, that headaches and buzzing of the ears assailed her, plunging her again into the world of silence.

However temporary it was, this miraculous cure was as predicted and seems to have very much encouraged the Bishop. Gathering together the some one hundred pages I had edited up to that time from my interview with members of the community and from consulting Sister's intimate journal, he decided to request a serious inquiry by theologians.

This cure proved to be the decisive factor which brought the Virgin of Yuzawadai to the knowledge of the public. One could no longer fail to recognize in the succession of the events of Yuzawadai the hand of Divine Providence.

The Meaning of the Miraculous Cure

As the angel predicted, the healing was provisional. It lasted only five months, but it nonetheless has a profound meaning.

I have already spoken of the problem posed by the Bishop on the reading of the manuscript which I had submitted to him from the notes of Sister Agnes. He was troubled indeed to know whether the third message given through the intermediary of the statue might not have been in some way a repeated version of all that had been reported to be the third secret of Fatima. It very much resembled those reports.

TRANSLATOR'S NOTE:

As previously noted the third secret of Fatima was never officially made public by the Church. Pope John XXIII was the first to open the secret in 1960 and he consulted his secretary and several cardinals who agreed with His Holiness that it not be made public. Subsequently, Paul VI, John Paul I and John Paul II held to the same decision. However, a priest who was on the commission for the beatification of the two younger children of Fatima gave out a version of the secret which was widely quoted and which does indeed very much resemble the third message of Our Lady at Akita.

Indeed Sister Agnes might have had knowledge of this because of leaflets at that time which might have come to her attention when she was catechist in the church of Myoko. But when I asked her about this she answered without ambiguity that she had never seen anything of this kind. However, the Bishop wanted to avoid any possible error even to the point of thinking to delete that part of the third message (concerning the chastisement).

It was precisely when the Bishop was thinking this that the hearing of Sister's ears took place on the 13th of October, anniversary of the message, and exactly in the manner the angel had predicted. It was a true authentication of the message. Indeed the grace of the healing could have been given on any day whatever. So why was it precisely on the 13th of October rather than another day? As I said I myself was projecting it for the last Sunday of October, and it was only afterwards that I understood why this date had been chosen.

Catholics of the entire world know well that the great miracle of Fatima took place on the 13th of October, which was also the last day of the apparitions. And the third secret given to Lucia would have been of such seriousness that it has not yet been made public. It gave place to more or less hypothetical versions which circulate just about everywhere in the world. Now at Akita it was also on the 13th of October that Mary warned us of a terrible chastisement which menaces the world. The witness says that the face of Our Lady, while remaining splendid, at that moment took on an expression of sadness.

115.

In order to prove the truth and the supernatural character of such a warning, a miraculous and tangible sign was necessary. This sign was given on that same day, October 13th, which will remain doubly memorable because it is at once the day of the message and the day of the healing.

The angel had predicted well when she announced that, *"The heart of those who doubt will melt and they will believe."* As said above, the doubts of the Bishop were dissipated thanks to the miracle of healing so that he decided to make no change in the text of the message and to submit it to examination by theologians.

†††

The International "Pilgrim Virgin" (Our Lady of Fatima) and the Miraculous statue of Our Lady of Akita. Bishop Ito said: "The message of Akita is the same as that of Fatima."

Chapter Ten

The Dream

We read in the preceding chapter that the angel made reference to a dream which Sister Agnes had had. Because of its meaning, I thought it best to give it special attention here.

On the morning of Monday, June the 10th, when I was going from the presbytery to the chapel for the 6 o'clock Mass, my glance was attracted by a bedcover hanging from one of the windows of the first floor. As it is rather rare to see bedding hanging from a window at such an early morning hour, it was natural that I noticed it. However, as it was a matter of no great importance I continued on my way and carried out the morning program as usual.

Now during dinner, one of the sisters began to speak of a terrible dream that Sister Agnes had had that morning. Curious to know more, I asked her to tell me about it in detail. Her voice was still deeply moved by emotion when she told me: "This morning I had a dream in which I was the victim of a terrible persecution to such extent that my heart was palpitating even after I awoke.

"Before me was a group of persons who seemed to be religious. One of them who must have been their head, a foreign Catholic theologian it seemed to me, had a gray colored habit and advancing towards me said in a peremptory tone: 'Why would the God of the Trinity be one God? We cannot believe that Christ is God. According to you, where then is the center of the Catholic faith? If you believe in God and say that you serve Him, why do you not do as we who adore a multitude of gods? If you say you believe in God, do as we; believe in many gods. Then all of us, too, will become Catholics. If you would join us, you would lead an easy and agreeable life as we do. It is indeed because you wish it that you lead that life there. You are truly painful to see. Go, tell us that the God of the Trinity is not one, that there are a multitude of gods. If not, take that for your pain.'

"Saying that, he brandished a sort of cane and I clearly saw that it was a large serpent which began to entwine itself around me. I was so afraid that I could not open my mouth but finally I was able to say with supreme effort: 'The God of the Trinity is the only God. I can believe in no other God than He. If you cannot believe that Christ is God, you can never become Catholics. I believe that the essential of the Catholic doctrine is that Christ is God and Man.'

"Then he returned to the charge: 'You say that Christ is God? We cannot believe that. You became a Catholic because you believe that Christ rose from the dead?'

"'Yes, that is true. It is because we believe that Christ is God and Man that we have become Catholics.'

"At this response the serpent tightened around me strongly and completely immobilized me. For moments he darted out his red and pointed tongue, bringing his nose before my face. I was too exhausted with fear and physical oppression to be able to answer to the same question which was tossed at me without ceasing like a defiance. I gripped my Rosary with all my strength reciting the prayers. When the serpent's red tongue came so close to my face I chased it with my Rosary, but my strength was little by little fading away. Seeking some aid around me, I saw my companions form a row on my right. I saw clearly that they were frightened and concerned, that they remained powerless to help me. Looking at each of them I could read in their look, 'We are with you, courage!' No one, even the superiors who are usually of such great help, was able to extend a helping hand.

"I was at the end of my strength, no longer able to chase the head of the serpent nor to say the prayers, when suddenly Father Yasuda appeared before me. He made a large Sign of the Cross saying: 'In the Name of the Father, of the Son, of the Holy Spirit.' Then he added in a strong voice, 'She has a right to say that we believe that the God of the Trinity is the only God. Those who do not wish to believe that cannot become Catholics.'

"At that moment the chief of the group who was standing at my left with his repugnant and menacing air began to recoil and then the serpent who held me prisoner also left.

"My companions were finally able to come to save me. I was in a state of extreme exhaustion. I did not even find enough energy to thank the chaplain for arriving in time.

Perspiration flowed abundantly, but I did not even have the courage to dry it. It is then that the guardian angel came and dried it for me.

"At that instant I awoke. All my body was really bathed in perspiration. 'Oh! It was not a dream,' I said to myself while trying to get up and at first not succeeding, so great was the oppression which still rested upon my breast. My hands and feet were cold and my voice did not succeed in giving off the slightest sound to call a neighbor to my help. When I looked at the clock it was past 4:30 in the morning.

"Once up, I saw that the perspiration had soaked through the sheet to the bed covering which still kept the imprint of my body. Seeing that, I hung it from the window until the sun would rise to dry it.

"In the chapel the dream continued to torment me and I begged the aid of the Lord to overcome my weakness. Here, when it came time for the common prayers, I was still too weak to be able to pray aloud.

"At first I decided not to speak of this dream to anyone but the fear was such that I ended up by whispering a word to my neighbor. She asked me what kind of dream it was but as we were having breakfast, I told her to wait a little. We went to pray before the Blessed Sacrament after which she came to my room and I told her what had happened. She told me with astonished air: 'You were right to be afraid. It is true, the bedding is still soaked.' You see, my Father, certainly it was to ask you to exercise discernment that this sister came to you to speak of it."

Such was the recital given to me by Sister Agnes concerning that dream. After hearing it to the end, I began by saying that certainly it could not have been a simple nightmare and I offered my personal interpretation:

"This does not concern only Sister Agnes. There seems to be here an allusion to the state of the Church and to certain of its orientations. The Church, in the name of evangelization, tries to approach other religions, even polytheists. At the same time it is set to accept compromises which draw the life of the faith into ways more adapted to the modern world, that is to say easier ways. It is clear that this attitude has some adherence even among those responsible in the Church. I believe it is our duty to observe faithfully the Word of God putting into it the best of ourselves, if we do not wish to be tricked in this fashion...

I was speaking to the community, and the sisters listened with attention, but some of them didn't seem to be taking the matter very seriously, "After all, it was only a dream," they said. Nevertheless, all were persuaded that this affair of the dream was over and would not be coming up again. If that were so, neither would I have made so much of it here, but as there had been so many external signs confirming the authenticity of the messages given through Sister Agnes in the past, so now something very extraordinary happened.

Now once again it is noteworthy that the entire community was involved... even as the community was to some extent "involved" in the actual dream itself. That very evening we all received a surprise!

After the Rosary which precedes evening prayers, Sister Agnes came abruptly to tell me: "Father, *there is a serpent in the next room!*"

I got up at once to go look in the parlor. Opening the door I saw an enormous serpent at the foot of the opposite wall. The sisters having also seen it from behind, I quickly closed the door, exhorting them to remain calm especially since the prayer had not finished. A little later I got the snake out and settled his account.

Sister Agnes told us that at the moment they were praying the invocation "Our Lady of the Holy Rosary, pray for us," the guardian angel appeared and told her, *"Tell the chaplain that there is a serpent in the next room at this moment. This is to give awareness to those who took your dream lightly. The chaplain will know how to guide you."* Surprised, she had interrupted her prayer to go and look. Carefully opening the door of separation, Sister Agnes discovered a serpent of the same large size as the one in her dream, lifting up his head and darting out its red tongue. It was then that she hastened to come and tell me.

So many years later the event may now seem simply an interesting story, but indeed it had the value of a warning in many ways. It was a premonitory sign.

Consider again the discourse of the chief of the group with his airs of a theologian. In the first question he asks why the Trinitarian God would be one God. Judaism had well believed in one God, Creator of Heaven and earth, but did not know the mystery of the Trinity. Without the revelation of this mystery it is not possible to believe that Jesus Christ is the unique Son of God. When the persecutor declares: "We cannot believe that Christ is God," he is saying nothing new; it is a problem which has grown with the increase of materialism and of scientism, deeply troubling souls. Actually it is an undeniable fact that atheism and materialism have penetrated even into the Church under diverse and disguised forms.

In the dream, a theologian throws into the face of the believer the defiance of materialism, expressing in a clear and simple fashion a true current of our time. With his friends, he would become a Catholic if the accused accepts to recognize the multitude of gods which, in the case of Japan, could refer to the numerous divinities of ancestral cult. It is an allusion to an easy way of evangelization which consists in not rejecting compromises with traditional beliefs. In conclusion he feigns compassion and proposes a bargain, "If you join us, you will be able to lead an easy and agreeable life with us," making of the faith a utilitarian complement to a life completely materialistic. In other words, it is the exaltation of the terrestrial life of man and the negation of the spiritual life which leads to God.

This episode cannot be treated lightly under the pretext that it is a dream. Indeed one can see in this the announcement of a trial which will affect Sister Agnes sometime later. It was without doubt to warn her of this event that the angel assured Sister Agnes saying, *"You spoke of the dream this morning at table, didn't you? Do not let it disturb you."* On the other hand one can say that it was to awaken the faith of those who did not give it attention, that a real serpent was placed before them.

TRANSLATOR'S NOTE:

As noted previously, it was the translator's intention to write a new book about the events of Akita based on this book of Father Yasuda and on other books, and omitting details like the above which are at once so extraordinary and yet may not seem so central to the great message for the world which Our Lady brought at Akita. But Bishop Ito gave a mandate first for the complete translation of Father Yasuda's book in its entirety and it was in the course of this work that the translator saw not only the wisdom of the Bishop, but, felt forced to exclaim: *"To what an extent God has gone in the events of Akita to draw our attention to the serious state of our times,* both within the Church and without, in order that we might know more exactly how to respond to Our Lady's terrible warning!"

Father Joachim Alonso, internationally celebrated theologian who was the official documentarian of Fatima, wrote a book on the third secret of Fatima in which he deduced that the secret referred above all to the struggles that would take place within the Church. He concluded that devotion to the Immaculate Heart of Mary was the great aid which God offered now to the world to save us from falling into the abyss.

We are obviously reminded of the words of Genesis recalling that She, the Immaculate Mother of the Savior, would be for each of us the one that would crush the head of the infernal serpent.

An Unexpected Visit

Bishop Ito had visited several renowned theologians of Japan and had given them my manuscript entitled "The Events Relative to the Virgin of Yuzawadai." Their reaction had been reserved if not to say negative. And without even going into the matter further they judged that a more profound inquiry was not necessary arguing that there was little material here for a theologian. Nevertheless, these inquiries resulted in drawing the attention of the public to what had previously been limited to whispered conversations.

On November the 3rd, 1974, the sisters received an unexpected telephone call from Tokyo. A journalist of the review *Catholic Graph* asked to come to the convent for an interview about the "Events which recently had been entertaining tittle-tattle." The sisters politely refused but without backing down.

While listening to them tell me their difficulties in discouraging such a prejudiced interviewer, while at the same time bound by the Bishop to absolute secrecy, I thought it was preferable to personally take the matter in hand. At that time the *Catholic Graph* was a review which seemed to be oriented towards denouncing all corruptions and abuses of religion and carried on a valiant combat for the renovation of Catholic environment.

In this matter in which we were confronted with supernatural events a little beyond good common sense, it did not seem advisable to leave the unbridled imagination of some journalists run wild. That would mean an open door to all kinds of misunderstandings. If erroneous information and fantasies circulated one could fear inauspicious consequences... not only in Catholic circles but in all of society.

Since I told the sisters that I would take responsibility for the interview, they were all out gathering stones for the Garden when the journalist arrived. He introduced himself saying that he had heard talk of the mysterious events concerning the statue of the Virgin in our convent and that he wished to know the truth, and for that he needed my cooperation. I then gave him the following brief summary of what had happened up to that time:

"First of all, in March of the previous year Sister Agnes had become suddenly deaf. After that she came to this convent, and later a wound similar to stigmata appeared on her left hand. At the dawn of the First Friday of July, she had gone to the chapel led by her guardian angel and saw the same kind of wound on the right hand of the statue of the Virgin. She received messages given through the intermediary of this statue from which she saw blood flowing from the wound, which was also witnessed by the other sisters."

My explanation seemed to be accepted without difficulty by the interviewer who shared the same faith. Even if he was not totally convinced, he no longer showed an attitude of rejection and I felt that his confidence was being gained little by little. When he promised to write a faithful account of what I had told him, I insisted that he first ask permission of the Bishop before publishing the article.

The latter was published almost immediately in the December issue of *Catholic Graph* under the title of: "The Virgin Mary Appears At Akita! The Truth Of The Matter." It was a first page story with photographs. The article began by describing the surroundings of the convent of the Institute of the Handmaids of the Eucharist and the author gave free reign to his imagination: "Before the war no one dared to tread the soil of this sacred mountain, calm and profound."

The following part, entitled "Under The Conduct Of The Angel," told about Sister Agnes hearing a first message while before the statue of the Virgin. There followed the encouragement to prayer in reparation for ingratitudes and the warning contained in the second and third messages. Finally, it passed in review the testimony of the sisters concerning the wound which appeared on the hand of the statue.

The article concluded that it is "impossible to affirm the actual state of things, whether the events of Akita are really miraculous." It added: "Nevertheless one thing is certain: only God is capable of performing miracles. That supposes that the meaning and the purpose of what happens, when there is a miracle, is worthy of consideration." Then citing my own words before concluding:

"As for the purpose or object of these apparitions, Father Yasuda explains first of all that 'To save the world today, it is necessary for those who believe to be aware of the urgency of prayer... the healing of Sister Agnes is the authentic proof of the messages. The wound in the form of the cross is another tangible proof... I intend to do all that I can to create in this place conditions favorable to prayer.'" (Reporting and text of Mr. Yoneda.)

Obviously *Catholic Graph* gave coverage of the events of Akita far beyond what had been expected. In addition to the report, they brought in an explanation of Mr. Queeny, who worked for the Tokyo television network, and the expert opinion of Father Nemshgy, both of whom presented the entire events of Akita as worthy of consideration. And, as the saying goes, this took off the lid.

Thus that which could have remained secret in a convent lost in the mountains suddenly became resounding news. And this act of Divine Providence was for us totally unexpected. Indeed it was only the beginning. Divine Providence ordained that in the year following there would be an event to draw still more public attention: the weeping of Our Lady's statue! Naturally criticism flared. The mockery of those who attributed this phenomena to human machinations and the voices of those who denied the supernatural character of the events, seemed to overwhelm the protest of believers who recognize the Hand of God with a simple faith. The clergy showed an indifferent attitude, if not negative, to the whole affair... and despite the official recognition of the supernatural origin of the events by the Bishop of the place, in April of 1984, many continued in an attitude of doubt or disbelief. As is written in the Bible, would the Virgin Mary also be a sign of contradiction?

But Our Lady was not finished. She had no intention of leaving us and the world in doubt.

Pilgrim Virgin of the World Apostolate of Fatima and Our Lady of Akita together in Akita, Nov., 1987

Chapter Eleven

The Statue Weeps

It was about 9 o'clock in the morning on January 4, (the first Friday) 1975. The spirits of all were still impregnated with the joyous atmosphere of the festivities which filled the first days of the New Year. I was in the presbytery when they ran to tell me: *"The statue of the Virgin is weeping!"*

Since this was the last day of a retreat which I was giving to the sisters I had begun to prepare the sermon, but I immediately put down my pen and went to see the statue.

It was normal to hope that some sign from Heaven would still happen in order to enable people to believe in the three messages given by Our Lady to Sister Agnes. I myself more or less was awaiting another miracle.

And as I reflect upon it well, this kind of prodigy, which no one in the world expected, is without doubt the most appropriate miracle for such a message. This touching grace from Heaven is in perfect harmony with the content of the messages, filling the heart at once with profound gratitude.

The notes and recollections of Sister Agnes, who was one of the first witnesses, recalls that first day when the statue wept: "It was the time of prayer which follows breakfast. Sister K., who was putting the chapel in order, came running to call me while I was still in the corridor, 'Agnes... come see!'

"Wondering what was happening, I followed her into the chapel. She pointed with her finger to the statue of the Virgin. 'What is it?' I asked her, looking at her face which had taken on an unearthly color. The pointing finger seemed like a trembling leaf. Approaching the statue I was shocked on seeing the face. Water was accumulating in the two eyes.

"'Oh! Water...' I said to myself when the water suddenly began to run down. 'Water which flows from the eyes... but then, those are tears!' I thought to myself: 'Could these be the tears of the Blessed Virgin?' I asked Sister K., but she remained fixed and her lips were trembling.

"Feeling my knees give way, I prostrated myself. Then coming to myself I said that something had to be done. I ran to the telephone to advise the Father who was in the presbytery at that moment. Then there was general astonishment. Father immediately arrived and all the community gathered in the chapel in the space of a few moments. Prostrated in the back, I did not have the courage to approach the statue. I prayed within myself with all my strength, 'Holy Mary, pardon me. It is I who have made you cry. Pardon! Lord, pardon me because I am a sinner.'

"Mary weeps because we have not taken count of all the graces obtained by Her intercession! I was abashed by the weight of regret.

"That day the tears appeared two more times. The second time was about one o'clock in the afternoon. As two of the sisters who were on retreat had to leave sooner, I went to gather medals placed in offering before the statue of Mary because I was sacristan that day. When I looked into the face of Our Lady to greet Her, after taking the medals from the table, I was amazed to see the tears again starting to flow. I felt myself shaken with an emotion still stronger than the first time, perhaps because I had discovered them myself and so close up. I took hold of myself and informed the sister who was at the other end of the chapel. And I hastened to tell the others. They all soon arrived with the Father and we recited the Rosary.

"At 4 o'clock Father Yasuda began his talk. I was touched when he explained that these tears were the authentic proof of the messages. The emotion which I had stifled until then suddenly overwhelmed me and I felt my body drained of all its energies. After the sermon, Father noticed that I was in such a weak state that I was unable to rise although my companions seemed to have thought simply that I was delaying to pray.

"The tears began to flow a third time while I was remaining thus for a long moment absorbed in prayer. Towards 6:30 in the evening, the sister who came to ring the dinner bell was the one who saw it first. The two of us were in the chapel praying. This time the tears did not flow by accumulation and then overflowing from the eyes. They streamed one after the other. It flowed, flowed... in a continual flux, they formed streams on the cheeks, the chin, down to the breast, and fell drop by drop.

"I found just the strength to prostrate myself, repeating in myself without being able to move my lips, 'Holy Mary, Holy Mary, why to such a degree?' The sisters who came seemed also deeply impressed. Even those who had remained perplexed the first two times, perhaps because they had not seen well, appeared convinced this time of the evidence of the miracle

"Meanwhile, the Bishop had arrived and seeing the tears for the first time, had cotton brought and he himself gradually dried the tears." Thus ends the detailed report from the intimate journal of Sister Agnes.

Twenty persons were witnesses of these three successive lachrymations. Ordinarily there would be less than ten sisters present in the convent, but members of other regional branches had joined us for the New Year retreat. As for myself, who had observed this phenomenon very closely each time, I was profoundly touched by it.

Both eyes of the wooden statue shone, liquid accumulated, overflowed, streamed, exactly as would tears from the eyes of a human being. Each one in turn spoke of it *as if being present at the tears of a living person.* The tears appeared on the inside edge of the eyes where lachrymal glands would be located, flowed along the nose, the cheeks, then fell drop by drop, exactly like a human person who would cry while maintaining the same position. The drops hesitated on the chin like little pearls, accumulated on the collar of the garment, rolled on the cincture, followed the foldings of the robe and fell down upon the globe.

Who would pretend to give a natural explanation to such a phenomenon? The scientific analysis of the liquid made immediately afterwards showed that it was indeed a question of "human tears." And when one sees liquid flowing from the eyes of a wooden statue, when the latter is so dry that it is already slightly cracked in some places, one cannot help but think that these are the true tears of Mary brought forth again by the creative power of God. Whether they believe in the supernatural nature of the facts or not, every witness who has seen this has been profoundly touched because they really had the impression of seeing Our Lady Herself crying. With time it seemed that some began to doubt. However, when one tries to deal with the miracle solely with the light of human intelligence one understands nothing and solves nothing; it is evident that the approach by human intelligence alone is the open door to skepticism.

If one considers that a miracle transcends all the laws of nature and could be caused only by the All Powerful God, to ask whether it is a question of a little miracle or a big miracle doesn't make sense. One can only bow before the mystery. For some time there were some people who not only took the facts lightly, but who even tried in every way to explain them away by such theses as "ectoplasmic faculties of Sister Agnes," even though there was not the slightest shred of support for such an affirmation.

In the following ten years, *scientific studies excluded any other explanation than the supernatural.* In my opinion, it is as impossible for a man to cause human tears to flow from a piece of wood as to change water into wine. I feel that here we are in the presence of a prodigy as unheard of as that at the marriage feast of Cana in the Gospel of John when Jesus transforms water into wine.

The statue had been carved from the hard wood of the Judea tree ten years before by M. Saburo Wakasa, a sculptor renowned in the area. It had completely dried out during the years since it was made and little cracks had begun to appear. It is already miraculous if water would flow from such material, but it is still more prodigious that a liquid slightly salty, *of the nature of true human tears,* should have *flowed precisely from the eyes.*

In the beginning, everyone was so amazed that no one thought of taking a picture, but this was done subsequently and the objective proof remained thus preserved. The lachrymations had begun on the 4th of January 1975, and they were succeeded at more or less regular intervals, sometimes day after day, until the 15th of September, 1981! The phenomenon occurred one hundred and one times! And it goes without saying that this never happened in exactly the same way as though in a stereotype scenario.

The quantity and manner was each time different as would be the case with human beings.

Reaction to the Mystery

If the eyewitnesses of the three lachrymations of the 4th of January showed more or less the same degree of astonishment, one nevertheless remarks great diversity in the final attitude of each one. And in such a case one is confronted, whether one wishes it or not, with an objective reality impossible to deny. When one finds oneself before a mystery which defies the laws of nature, after the first astonishment one asks what such a mystery could mean. And the more disconcerting the fact, the more one looks for the true reason. When that appears to be a sign coming from God, one needs to exercise prudent discernment with a disposition of profound veneration.

When some marvel is produced through skillful human artifice (such as a magic act) forgetfulness soon gives way to the first reaction of surprise. Furthermore, mystic theologians say that if the marvels come from a diabolical action, the surprise felt in the beginning diminishes with time without exercising lasting influence on the spirit.

In summary, when it is a question of Divine Intervention it necessarily carries a profound meaning in relation to the "sign" given by Heaven and man conforms to the Will of God in recognizing it as such. These signs do not contradict the Gospel. They bring home to us the promise made by Jesus: *"I am with you until the end of the world."*

What then are the first interpretations given to the "tears of the Virgin?"

Words of the Angel

As we have already seen, Sister Agnes who discovered the tears the second time, remained prostrated because of her emotion, incapable of moving. Even after the last Benediction of the Blessed Sacrament which closed the retreat of the New Year, she was unable to rise and she sent one of the sisters to ask the Bishop and myself to come to the chapel.

Later we had her write down for us exactly what she told us at that moment: "During the Rosary after the talk,* I again saw the guardian angel who had not appeared for a long time (it was the first time since the curing of my deafness) and she said the Rosary with me." Then she disappeared for a moment, returning during the prayer of silence a little after the profession of the lay members.

"She told me: '*Do not be so surprised to see the Blessed Virgin weeping. She weeps because She wishes the conversion of the greatest number; She desires that souls be consecrated to Jesus and to the Father by Her intercession.***

"'*He who directs you told you during the last sermon today; your faith diminishes when you do not see. It is because your faith is weak. The Blessed Virgin rejoices in the consecration of Japan to Her Immaculate Heart because She loves Japan. But She is sad to see that this devotion is not taken seriously.** Even though She has chosen this land of Akita to give Her messages, the local pastor doesn't dare to come for fear of what one would say. Do not be afraid. The Blessed Virgin awaits you all, Her hands extended to pour forth graces. Spread devotion to the Virgin. She rejoices in the profession of the lay members consecrated today by Her intercession in conformity to the spirit of your Institute. You must not consider the lay members thus consecrated as of little importance. The prayer which you have the custom of saying, 'Grant to Japan the grace of conversion through the intercession of the Virgin Mary,' is pleasing to the Lord.*

"'*You who have believed while seeing the tears of Mary, when you have permission of your superior speak to the greatest number in order to console the hearts of Jesus and Mary. Spread this devotion with courage for Their greater glory.*

"'*You will transmit my words to your superior and to him who directs you.*' She leaned forward to look at me and then disappeared.

---

*Sister Agnes is referring to the last talk of the retreat given by Father Yasuda which had preceded the Rosary and the closing Benediction.

**For further explanation of this very important message see *The Meaning of Akita*.

The first words of the angel, *"Do not be surprised,"* appear like an encouragement and an exhortation to the sister who remained prostrate without moving at sight of the tears. The angel then explains that the tears of Our Lady were shed to ask the conversion of the greatest number. When she adds, *"Mary weeps because She wishes that souls be consecrated to Jesus and to the Father through Her intercession,"* the angel insists on the urgency of the request.

With regard to the profession of the lay members, the angel assures us that souls consecrated in conformity with the spirit of the Institute please the heavenly Father and His Son. She warns us against considering this act of consecration lightly. The consecration to Mary which leads us to Jesus, Jesus leading us to the Father and to the Holy Trinity, is in conformity with the teaching and tradition of the Church.

It is touching that Mary had indeed chosen this land of Akita to spread Her graces upon Japan which She desires so much to lead to the faith. Is this not the grace called forth by the blood and tears of a multitude of martyrs since the coming of Saint Francis Xavier four centuries before?

But this is not a message only for Japan. It applies to all the world which has been consecrated to the Immaculate Heart of Mary, and especially to nations which have been consecrated, as well as individuals. *Each must make the consecration effective.*

Reaction

On Monday January 6th, two years later, there was the New Year's reunion of all the priests of the district of Akita which I attended in the company of Bishop Ito. After having passed in review all the subjects on the agenda one of the priests said: "I have heard speak of lachrymations of the statue of the Virgin and I do not know what to think. Bishop, could you give us your opinion?"

And another, without waiting for the Bishop's answer, said: "In our time, this kind of event interests no one. One would be much better to be completely quiet concerning it." For him it was something to be filed away.

Another priest spoke: "When I did my theology I chose the Virgin Mary as the subject of study. This led me to read the works of numerous Fathers of the Church on the matter. I noticed two things: at that time the dogma of the Assumption had not yet been promulgated, but I had become certain that one day this would take place. The second thing concerns the question of Mary, Mediatrix of all graces. This is not yet a dogma, but I have understood little by little that in the near future it will be.

"When I heard that blood had flowed from the statue I remembered having once seen a red and salty liquid, like resin, sweat from the surface wood that was several years old. I concluded that that must have been the case here. But for tears, it is difficult to find a satisfactory explanation and I rather tend to believe that this is something supernatural. This said, as long as one has no scientific proof of the nature of this liquid, one cannot affirm with certitude that there was truly a Divine Intervention." Finally the Bishop himself spoke: "I had seen the wound on the hand of the statue and the blood flow, but I was much more impressed when I dried the tears which flowed from the eyes. I truly felt that I was in the presence of a miracle."

Gradually as the most diverse opinions were voiced one after the other, I came to a decision. It was necessary to find scientific proof. Shortly afterwards, I went to seek the counsel of Professor Okuhara of the faculty of medicine of Akita. I showed him the bandages which had served to sponge the blood six months before and the cotton used to dry the tears of the 4th of January. On his recommendations I asked Professor Sagisaka of the Faculty of Legal Medicine* to make a rigorous scientific examination.

It goes without saying that we did not tell him the origin of the liquids submitted for examination in order not to harm the objectivity of the studies. After two long weeks of waiting the following results were communicated to me:

The matter adhering on the gauze is human blood. The sweat and the tears absorbed in the two pieces of cotton are of human origin.

---

*The Faculty of Legal Medicine refers to a medical examiner, a pathologist.

The objects submitted to this scientific examination reveal the presence of strange bodies due to the contact of the fingers which had used the gauze and cotton to absorb the blood and tears. But this had no bearing upon the result.

Furthermore (and this was an amazing fact for one who knew the actual origin of the materials) when the blood was examined it was found to belong to group B, and the sweat and tears belonged to group AB. Now it is unthinkable and scientifically impossible that the same person belong to different groups.

The reason for this soon became apparent. It will be recalled that the supernatural nature of these events was the theory of ectoplasm, which suggested that Sister Agnes in some mysterious way transmitted her own blood "through the air" to the statue. However unreasonable it sounds, it is amazing how this completely unsupported theory dampened faith.

And this happened because when the scientific results were published, the *Catholic Graph* in a first article pointed out that the blood was group B. And Sister Agnes belongs to this same group. In a second article they ignored the fact that the tears belonged to group AB, preferring to retain a "certain coherence with the preceding article."

Thus the first commission inquiring into the supernatural character of the events did not know that the tears belonged to group AB, and thus had extended their theory to conclude that Sister Agnes had, by an ectoplasmic power, transferred both her blood and tears to the statue. In reality, it was a hasty conclusion refuted by the reality of the events. Truth cannot be stifled by arguments which at first appear satisfying, but which do not stand up under serious analysis.

Was there indeed anything more Heaven could have done to remove all argument and to convince the world? Sometime later, on August 22nd 1981 (Feast of Our Lady Queen of the World) tears again flowed from the statue. This resulted in even more solid scientific confirmation as we shall soon see.

†††

Chapter Twelve

The Virgin and Saint Francis Xavier

On August 15th, 1549, Feast of the Assumption of the Virgin Mary, Saint Francis Xavier, messenger of the good news of Jesus Christ, landed in Japan for the first time at the port of Kagoshima. It is a recorded historic fact. By an effect of Divine Providence the Virgin wished that this precise day be the one for the people of Japan to first meet Christianity. And it goes without saying that this event led, through the blessing and grace of God, to an impressive number of vocations in our country.

When he set foot on this corner of the Japanese archipelago, Francis Xavier certainly did not fail to show his love and devotion to the Virgin Mary who had preserved him from dangers through a most perilous crossing. Beyond doubt he consecrated Japan to Her Immaculate Heart and prayed for her conversion on this solemnity when Mary is honored in Her greatest glory.

I remember having seen a film in my younger years on the discovery of America by Christopher Columbus. I vividly remember the moving scene in which the troop of navigators humbly kneels in prayer on the banks of the unknown country where their boat has landed.

It is unthinkable that a saint like Francis Xavier, driven by an ardent missionary zeal, would not have made a fervent prayer of supplication to the Lord and asked Mary to intercede for the success of his mission on this blessed day, the Feast of Her Assumption. As a matter of fact, the prayer of the saint and the help of Mary from the very beginning had remarkable effects on the evangelization of Japan. However, terrible persecutions followed shortly afterwards on the part of the rulers and there began a tragic period without precedent in the history of Japan marked by executions and tortures without number.

If the tears of Mary were not visible to the eyes of men at that time, is it not certain that they mixed with the multitude of so many martyrs whose blood reddened the land of the Rising Sun?

The Martyrs of Akita

Recalling the words of the angel addressed to Sister Agnes: *"The Virgin has chosen this land of Akita to give Her messages,"* I looked into a book relating the history of the martyrs of Akita in the hope of finding some witness to the seeds of grace which could have been sown during those years of suffering. I will recite a brief passage from the remarkable study of Mr. Tetsujo Muto, entitled *History of the Christians of Akita: Snow, Blood, and Holy Cross:*

"The third of June in the first year of the Kan'ei era (1624) marked the beginning of the sad history of the Christians of Akita. On this day took place the first executions in the fiefdom."

The book goes on to quote from the journal of Masakage, young brother of the judge of the castle, who was a person feared by all the Christians as though the devil in person. In this journal Masakage records the three things he did on June the 3rd: "One, I left the castle with my musket. Two, I had 32 Christians burned, 20 of them men and 12 women. Three, it was a nice day."

The book continues: "This is the only living chronicle which has come down to us concerning the genocide perpetrated against the Japanese Christians in this region at the beginning of the 17th century."

One is profoundly shocked by the last words "It was a nice day," whose cruel echo comes down to us despite the separation of three centuries. At the same time, the reader sees rolling on before his eyes the sacrifice of some dozens of crucified suffocating on the gibbet in the midst of the flames and fire which mount towards the heavens under leaden sky...

Crasset recalls the scene in his work *History Of Christianity In Japan:* "When the believers had been brought to the place of suffering, they were attached one by one to stakes which had been set in the ground a little apart from each other. Kindling wood was placed around them and set afire. With a single heart and a single soul they called upon the Lord the Savior while raising their eyes to Heaven and accomplishing their martyrdom. The bodies were kept for three days by some men.

"Strange to say, certain guards began to say that the sky was illuminated during the night. One of them advised some believers and all wished to see the mysterious phenomenon, going even to pass the night on the roofs of houses. The third evening, a large cloud covered the sky and a heavy rain fell on more than 300 persons gathered at the places. These events brought great comfort to the Christians, and the pagans were amazed to see such prodigies take place before their eyes.

"When John Kiemon was tied to the stake, a manuscript fell from his pocket. What was written upon it reveals to us the depth of his devotion towards the Virgin Mary:

"'Holy Virgin, filled with Divine grace, it is through Your Maternal tenderness that a being as unworthy as I has been able to believe in Your Son Jesus Christ and to render Him homage.

"'Deign to preserve my wife and my children from the sufferings of hell and preserve us in the faith until death.

"'Holy Mother, in my so great weakness how will I find the courage to bear by myself the great trial? Grant me by the grace of your Divine Son the strength to overcome my fear. I do not beg help because of fear of falling into hell. My only desire is to offer myself in holocaust in the flames of the wood. Very good Mother, do not disdain my prayers and deign to protect our wives, our children, and all our companions that they may remain firm in the faith and in the Holy Doctrine until the hour of death.

"'My soul experiences an ardent desire for the Holy Doctrine preached and cultivated without surcease by the priests of Japan. I am aware of the daring of such a request, but I know also that Jesus, from the height of the cross, gave us Mary for a Mother. That is why, despite my fear, I come to implore Your help.'"

It is certainly not by chance that Mary chose this land of Akita, reddened by the blood of so many martyrs, to give Her message and to manifest Her tears. The angel continues with the assurance:

"Do not fear. The Blessed Virgin awaits you all, Her hands extended to distribute graces."

How can we fail to lend an attentive ear to such a warm invitation?

The Second Evangelization of Japan

Two hundred and eighty years after this sad page in Christian history, Father Faucade of the foreign missions of Paris arrived in Japan and laid the foundations of a new evangelization. Landing at the Port of Naha on May 1st, 1844, he celebrated Mass in the infirmary of a war ship. After a prayer of thanksgiving, he consecrated Japan to the Immaculate Heart of Mary. The text of that prayer of Consecration is reported to us by Father Wasaburo Urakawa in the first volume of *Resurrection of the Christians:*

"Oh, most Holy Heart of Mary, most beautiful, most pure, most honorable, stainless fountain of goodness, of sweetness, of compassion and of love, throne of all virtues, heart most tender and worthy of praises and above all except the Divine Heart of Jesus, to You who have confided to me, despite my extreme weakness, the charge of spreading the Gospel in these islands, I present and consecrate them in so far as it is possible in order that You may take them under Your special protection.

"When the work of evangelization will have begun in such a way that a solid base will have been made with a sufficient number of persons snatched from their vain idols and gained to the Christian faith and a chapel constructed, I promise at once to send a request to the Holy See in Rome in order that the entire country may be placed under Your protection by public and official act.

"Oh, most merciful Heart of Mary, Heart most powerful with the Sacred Heart of Jesus so that it has never been heard or known that anyone who has sought Your protection has been abandoned, do not despise my humble prayers. Make my heart ever better, dissipate the fog which holds it in darkness. Confronted by great difficulties and great dangers, I come to implore the graces of humility, prudence, intelligence, and courage. Since the All-Powerful and Very Compassionate God, Father Son and Holy Spirit, has chosen the miserable person I am according to what is written: What is despised by the world, God has chosen: that which is not to bring to nothing that which is, (1 Corinthians 1: 28)... in order that He may deign to bring the light of the Gospel and to eternal life this people plunged for several centuries into darkness and death. Amen."

It was only shortly afterwards that Japan put an end to its policy of closed borders and at the same time the long persecutions of Christians came to an end. Nevertheless, Christianization did not progress. The faith spread but slowly and the missions remained almost without effect.

Then came the war in the Pacific which was a catastrophe without precedent in the history of the Japanese people. It ended with the disaster of Hiroshima and Nagasaki and the *capitulation of August 15, 1945*, Feast of the Assumption. For the some ninety thousand Catholics of this country, it was a coincidence willed by Divine Providence which would suggest once again the close link of their country with the Virgin Mary. With common accord the assembly of Japanese bishops, following the example of Father Faucade, of whom we have spoken above, decided to consecrate the nation to the Immaculate Heart of Mary and encourage this devotion among the Catholics.

On the 4th of January, 1975, when the statue wept three times, the angel said to Sister Agnes: *"The Holy Virgin rejoices in the consecration of Japan to Her Immaculate Heart because She loves Japan. But She is sad to see that this devotion is not taken seriously."* Filial love towards Mary, Mother of God and given to be Mother of all humanity, has always been considered as a devotion among the most orthodox throughout the ages with a foundation in tradition as well as in scripture. Sustained by the love of Mary, the Christians of whom we have spoken resisted cruel persecutions and were able to consummate their martyrdom. Such has always been the love of the Virgin for Japan and Her attachment to the Japanese people.

But then what is the meaning of those tears shed today?

The "Prayer Of Consecration of Japan to the Immaculate Heart of Mary" is found on page 241 of the collection of prayers used in all the Catholic churches of Japan. But if one could borrow the penetrating look of the angel to see into these same churches, would one find many Christians turning to that page? Or even if it is not said orally, in how many churches can one find a faithful devotion to Mary animated by this intention?

TRANSLATOR'S NOTE:

Readers of this book outside of Japan may easily apply almost every word above to themselves and to their own nation. Following the appeal of Our Lady of Fatima, *most countries* have been consecrated to the Immaculate Heart of Mary, and the entire world has five times been consecrated to the Immaculate Heart of Mary by the Holy Father, most recently on March 25, 1984, *in union with all the bishops of the world.* And yet indeed, how many even think of this consecration, let alone try to understand what it really means and how it applies to each one individually? This is critical in the messages of Our Lady of Fatima and at Akita. As Pope John Paul II explains, the consecration means an entrustment of ourselves to Mary (even as Our Lord entrusted us to Her from the Cross) and *bringing the reality of this entrustment into our lives* by such devotions as the Scapular and the Rosary. Also these tears of Our Lady in Japan should have a special meaning for everyone in the United States, the nation which destroyed Nagasaki and Hiroshima with the atomic bomb, ending the Pacific War on the Feast of the Assumption in 1945. The economic ties today between the U. S. and Japan are such that despite the great distance between the two nations there are cultural and economic ties all the more amazing because of the wounds of war which preceded them.

ttt

We live in a time when it is not rare to see all prayers of petition through the intercession of Mary taken lightly. There are even persons who protest about superstition and even heresy. And before subjecting such cries to the proof of argument, one must say that such proposals are a flagrant rupture with the official position of the Church.

Vatican Council II announced clearly regarding Marian devotion: "All Christians must pray to Mary, Mother of God and Mother of men, in order that She may continue to intercede today with Her Divine Son in the communion of all the saints because Mary, by Her fervent supplication, helped the Church from its beginning and is elevated above all the angels and all the saints." Doesn't Our Lady weep because this text of the Council has been left almost in complete oblivion? The angel follows with these words of encouragement: *"The prayer that you are accustomed to* say, 'Grant to Japan the grace of conversion through the intercession of theVirgin Mary,' is pleasing to the Lord." In the convent of the Handmaids of the Eucharist, this prayer is recited every day before the Rosary in the presence of the Blessed Sacrament exposed.

This prayer which we have the custom of saying each day in our community, which finds its origin in Saint Francis Xavier, was repeated some time later by Father Faucade and reformulated in a recent time by the Assembly of Japanese Bishops. Full of filial tenderness and confidence one does not fail to recite it with ever renewed devotion.

TRANSLATOR'S NOTE:

Bishop Ito asked for the translation of this book and its promulgation in the world because he was convinced that the message of Our Lady of Akita is not only for Japan but for every nation. However, as Our Lady exhorts the people of Japan to recall their consecration to Her Immaculate Heart as a nation, so each of us should pray for our own countries and weep and make reparation for our own national sins and our own lack of response to this critical message from Heaven, recalling that the chastisement of which Our Lady speaks threatens every nation, and that Our Lady has been appointed by God to save us and bring us peace. She said this explicitly in Her message of Akita as She has said it at Fatima. In the words of Jacinta, *"God has entrusted the peace of the world to Her."* In Our Lady's own words, "If My requests are heard... an era of peace will be granted *to mankind."*

✝✝✝

Chapter Thirteen

The Requested Sacrifice

Sister Agnes lost her hearing on the 16th of March, 1973. For a time after the morning call, she did not speak to anyone and was not aware of the abnormal state of her ears. When the telephone rang about 6:30 in the morning the sound had seemed somewhat distant. When she took up the phone she could hardly distinguish the voice at the other end (a sister was calling from the mother house of Akita). Then suddenly she was again plunged into that world of silence. The events which followed during the next ten years little by little opened her eyes to the profound meaning of this trial which was the work of Divine Providence.

At the moment it happened, it was like a catastrophe for her and forced her to leave the catechetical service which had been going so well and to come and take refuge in this place of peaceful prayer lost in the fullness of nature. At that time the community was small and rarely received visitors. All the sisters were of one heart in prayer and daily work. When Sister Agnes took up her work of sewing in her own room, she joined a prayer with each movement of the needle, never detaching her thoughts from the Lord. Thus without her being aware of it at all, her faith was being purified in the crucible of trial and her heart invited to the greatest intimacy with the Lord, in order that she might become a pliable instrument capable of receiving the messages of Mary.

The series of events which we have traced in the previous pages, and the message which is at their heart, began shortly after Sister Agnes became deaf. The importance of this trial was underlined by Our Lady Herself in Her first words: *"Is your deafness painful to bear? You will be cured, be sure. Be patient... pray in reparation for the sins of humanity..."* These simple words conceal an entire instruction.

What are we searching for in life in our time, whoever we are? It can be summed up in two words: temporal happiness. One finds a reason for living in the pleasures of the world. One lives for diversion, leisure, an easy life, to such a point that one sees in work only the means of obtaining leisure. The search for pleasure for the body, the banishment of pains and anguish of the spirit, become the ultimate ends of life. And when these conditions cannot be realized, it is common practice to brandish slogans of social justice or respect for the rights of man while declaring war on other men.

Carried on the wave of contemporary fashion, Christians have more and more difficulty living the faith as a total offering to God, of *offering the sufferings and sacrifices of each day* in reparation for sins, an offering nevertheless inherently *necessary to the economy of salvation.* Certainly it is not easy to remain serene and to withhold oneself entirely from the influence of the overwhelming flood of materialism which seems to carry all before it, even when one clings to the Catholic faith and tries to live it with the help of grace.

One does not accept the least suffering or the least effort if these are not paid for in some way by a temporal satisfaction. The old proverb, "No good without pain," seems to be effaced from our memories. To bear moral pain and physical suffering in a spirit of offering and of love for God, patient acceptance of His Will, is an attitude long since relegated to the museum of alien follies of religion.

When one looks at the Cross from this angle, one can easily understand the dispositions of the crowd laughing at this pure sacrifice of expiation: "If you are the Messiah, come down from the Cross and save Yourself!" Those of us who live following the tastes of our time, do we not in a certain way take up this insulting cry of the crowd? Dazzled by the needs of the world, do we forget the needs of the Kingdom and forget to look for the Divine Will?

We do not like the sacrifices asked of us and seek by every means to avoid the efforts which come our way. And if we hook on to the little happiness of the moment, do we not finish by making it a reason for being alive one day to the other and lose our true sense of the Christian religion to which we thought ourselves attached? In this perspective, the trial of the deafness which affected Sister Agnes, even if the causes were natural, merits that we study it with a special attention.

We have already spoken of the details of her miraculous cure, although provisional, which took place on the 13th of October, 1974. This cure had been announced on the 18th of May. Let us consider again the angel's words: "*Your ears will be restored in August or in October; you will hear, you will be healed. But that will last for only a moment, because the Lord still wishes this offering, and you will become deaf again. And seeing that your ears hear again, the heart of those who still doubt will melt and they will believe. Have confidence and pray with good intentions.*"

Later, in the message of September 22, the angel described in detail the circumstances in which the cure would take place. Then she adds in order that Sister Agnes might understand well that this will be provisional: "*Your ears will hear for only a certain time, they will not be completely healed, you will become deaf again. The Lord still wishes this offering...* "

When we realized that Sister Agnes had really been cured we were amazed and we all expressed to her our sincere joy. But this was, despite everything, mitigated because we knew that if her ears had been healed in the way predicted, they would also be closed again. And one could not help but wonder with a certain anxiety, as she did, just how long it would last. One had the impression that this might be shortly afterwards, and putting things in the best light, one could also think that the delay would be shorter even than hoped for.

On Thursday, the 6th of March, 1975, I was in the process of transporting an enormous stone of several tons, with the help of four workers, which I had chosen for the Garden of Mary. We were moving it by sled on the snow. Towards midday, hearing the voice of a sister who called me from the convent, I ran thinking it must be the telephone only to learn that the statue of the Virgin was weeping.

It had not wept since the 4th of January, two months before. I hastened to the chapel in my work clothes and when I was close to the statue, I saw that the wood was wet near the feet and that a drop remained on the bottom of the chin. While I was noting this, the Bishop arrived and saying that one could not be sure without touching it, he gathered the drop on his index finger where it shone, visible to the eyes of all.

At this precise moment one heard the noise of a taxi arriving at the entrance of the convent and there was the journalist from the *Catholic Graph!* Not wishing to let pass such an opportunity, he hastened to take out his camera but the photo showed nothing because the tears had just stopped. If I had not recalled this incident before, it is because there was nothing else in particular except that it was the first lachrymation after the three which took place on January the 4th.

However, it was from *this* day that Sister Agnes began to experience violent headaches without anyone at first knowing. During Mass of the First Friday of the month and on the First Saturday, it redoubled in intensity to the point that she remained prostrate holding her neck in her hands after Communion. She refused to come for breakfast and kept her prostrate position without moving. Later she came to see me and said: "I no longer hear anything, as the angel had predicted. The angel looked at me with a compassionate air and said: '*Support that, until the time willed by the Father*,' and then disappeared."

Sister Agnes had a presentiment on the previous evening with a headache. She relates that it was of the same nature as the headaches with which she was assailed before her first deafness. It was not only a feeling of heaviness, but she felt oppressed as if one had placed a steel pot over her head with a deafening roar which resounded as though in a tunnel or near a jet plane taking off.

I took her the same day to the Municipal Hospital of Akita and to the specialist of the Hospital of the Red Cross. The Municipal Hospital delivered the following medical certificate: "One must fear a brutal lowering of hearing in both ears. First consultation 7th of March, 1975. Must observe relative rest and undergo a treatment for the moment. (signature)" The Red Cross Hospital gave the following diagnosis: "Bad hearing of both ears. Annex: Following the fall of auditive faculties, the level of perception has been null even in regulating the apparatus to the maximum. A regaining of the auditive faculties in the future is highly improbable. I certify the above. (Date and signature.)" Thus Sister Agnes found herself plunged into a world cut off from all sound from this day on, as it happened two years before. And what is more, the doctors declared it incurable after having submitted her to minute examinations.

However, as the angel had declared: "*You will not hear for a certain time... you will not yet be completely cured,*" it was permitted to hope that she would be cured definitely one day and all hope was not lost. Moreover, the angel had encouraged her to accept this with patience, "*Until the time willed by the Father.*" None of us knew the day nor the hour, but all hearts were united in prayer strengthened with a new hope.

It is fitting that we should again take up our reflection on the meaning of the mysterious events concerning the statue. We have already seen that a miracle is never given without a spiritual reason. Magicians do their tricks to astonish spectators, but God does not turn over the laws of nature for the pleasure of amazing men.

Why the blood, the sweat, the perfume, the hundred and one times that the statue wept? We have already said that these signs were given to verify the supernatural character of the messages, messages given through the intermediary of the statue and of ears mysteriously closed and then miraculously opened, closed again... with the promise of a final cure.

To sum up we can say that the first message is a greeting and encouragement addressed to the Sister; the second is an invitation to sacrifice and prayer offered to appease the anger of the Father; finally, the third is a warning against eventual chastisement and an exhortation to confidence in Our Mother in Heaven. And perhaps the following words of the second message constitute the essential of the entire message: "*Many men in this world afflict the Lord. I seek souls to console Him. To appease the anger of the Celestial Father, I seek, with my Son, souls who repair by their suffering and their poverty for sinners and ingrates.*"

Many men in this world afflict the Lord... one could say that the actual state of the world is such that it appears to be the contemporary version of the Way of the Cross made by the Savior. In our day there is practically no man who has not heard speak of Christ. One knows His name, one has met Him in one way or another. And does not the great contemporary mass have the same attitude towards Him as the Jews of two thousand years ago? There was no one to console the Savior. One is, above all, preoccupied with consoling oneself. Can one hear anything other than shouts of injury and of mockery? *"I seek souls to console the Master."* What a poignant appeal!

Are we not being asked if we wish to console the Master? To run to His help on the road of Calvary and, like Veronica who courageously offered a towel to dry the face of the Lord, to brave the prejudices and the oppositions of the entourage and to approach and participate with all of our being in the Holy Sacrifice?

We must recognize that believers themselves are fooled by current fashion... flight before suffering, frantic searching for pleasure... and end by renouncing the Cross. One wishes a Christianity without a cross, which accommodates us with salvation in sweetness and without much effort.

Is it not because of this sad state of things that Our Mother has manifested tears so many times? And what is going to happen if we continue to pass over the dangerous warnings, feigning indifference despite the miracle of seeing tears flowing from a statue of wood?

In the first chapter of Saint Luke one finds this impressive passage: While Zachary, who will be the father of John the Baptist, precursor of Jesus, is incensing the altar in the temple the Archangel Gabriel appears to announce that his wife Elizabeth is going to conceive a son. As he did not immediately believe, the angel declares, "I have been sent to you to announce this good news. But you will no longer be able to speak until it happens. Indeed you have not believed my words which will be fulfilled on the fixed day."

Sister Agnes did not become deaf because she doubted the words of the angel. Rather her ears were cured, as the angel predicted, because she at once believed. It is important to note that God punished Zachary for his lack of faith in the angel's word by sending a physical trial.

Numerous famous examples show that God permits the direct intervention of angels when events of great importance are involved, as is the case here. The numerous manifestations of the angels and the miracles which took place at Yuzawadai are undeniable facts. Furthermore, God willed that not only angels, but *the Blessed Virgin Herself appear in person to transmit Her messages. And She did this in a poignant manner... weeping.* When men on earth join sobs and flowing tears to their laments, they find brethren to run to their aid, to loyally hear them.

After so pathetic an appeal from their Mother in Heaven, how many times will it be necessary for men to become aware of the gravity of the moment and to make honorable amendment?

Attach Great Importance To This Day

Saturday, May 1st, 1976, was the Feast of Saint Joseph, patron of workers. On that day we were awaiting eleven visitors coming from Tokyo. Some men of advanced age, dwelling in the suburb west of Tokyo for the most part, had formed a group which they called Anshinkai with the purpose of deepening their faith while at the same time carrying on their professional activities in society. I had transferred the Mass that day to the evening so they would be able to participate and pray with the sisters. Thus Lauds had been followed by a time of adoration that morning, without Mass.

After breakfast Sister Agnes went to the chapel and saw that the tears were flowing again from the statue. The previous lachrymation had been one year and two months before, namely the 6th of March of the preceding year. Naturally, everyone went to the chapel and we recited a Rosary.

Then when Sister K. came about twenty after nine to make a sketch on drawing paper, she found to her astonishment that the tears had begun again and immediately informed all the others who again gathered to recite a Rosary with her. I could not be present at this second lachrymation because I left to give some courses in the city. I was told about it when I returned a little before midday.

A half hour before vespers, which was scheduled for 5 o'clock in the afternoon, one of the sisters went to the chapel and again the statue was weeping. A third Rosary was recited by the entire community.

The group of visitors arrived later than expected, towards 8 o'clock in the evening. We had been awaiting without eating because the Mass had to precede the dinner. Taking advantage of the holidays in the month of May, about twenty other persons were expected to arrive from Niigata, Sendai, and other regions.

The Mass which began at 8 o'clock was said in honor of Saint Joseph to thank him and to ask his protection. It ended about 9 o'clock. When everybody had left the holy place, I remarked that Sister Agnes remained alone, prostrate without moving since the end of her Communion. A little later she came to find me with a paper grasped in her hand. The angel had appeared to her after Communion. This is the text:

"Many men in this world afflict the Lord. Our Lady awaits souls to console Him. Remain in poverty, sanctify yourself and pray in reparation for the ingratitudes and the outrages of so many men. The Rosary is your weapon. Say it with care and more often for the intention of the Pope, of bishops and priests.

"You must not forget these words (of Mary). The Blessed Virgin prays continually for the conversion of the greatest possible number and weeps, hoping to lead to Jesus and to the Father souls offered to Them by Her intercession. For this intention, and to overcome exterior obstacles, achieve interior unity, form a single heart. Let believers lead a life more worthy of believers! Pray with a new heart.

"Attach great importance to this day for the glory of God and of His Holy Mother. With courage spread this devotion among the greatest number. Inform your superior and him who directs you of what I have told you." Saying this the angel disappeared.

After reading this I went to dinner at the presbytery with the group of visitors. About twenty minutes of ten in the evening we were still at table and they were recording some of the happenings of their trip (they had traveled 700 kilometers by car). The telephone rang. It was a call from the convent. The statue of Mary was again weeping for the fourth time in the same day!

Through the dark night we all hastened to the chapel and at the sight of the tears flowing from the eyes of the statue some prostrated themselves, others sobbed, each manifesting his emotion in a different way. As on the other occasions, I took out my Rosary and we meditated on the Sorrowful Mysteries.

During the recitation of the Rosary, the tears continued to flow abundantly from both eyes down the cheeks; the drops fell from the chin to the breast and even wet the pedestal. They finally stopped during the second decade.

Among the visitors who had come to spend the night at the convent, beginning with the twenty persons who were not a part of the Tokyo group, it seems that certain ones had the suspicion that there was some kind of fakery inside the statue. The next day, the third Sunday of Easter, I cited the words of the angel quoted above during my sermon and invited everyone present to reflect on the meaning of the tears shed by Our Lady. That day there were still many more visitors including four doctors. While we were dining in a warm and animated ambiance, the same news of the previous evening came to cut short our conversations. It was about 12:30.

Almost at once the chapel was full. This time even those who had not been able to repress suspicions the evening before began to weep and sob. The doctors present agreed that this could only be a prodigy. According to the records of the community, there were 55 eyewitnesses that day.

The tears had flowed five times in two days, leaving for the first time visible traces even on the cheeks after the tears disappeared. They are still visible today despite the time that has since passed.

Witnesses

Afterwards, eleven of the men from Tokyo participated in an interview for the *Catholic Graph* in the name of all the eyewitnesses of these days. Their testimony was reproduced later in a work entitled *"Messages of a Heavenly Voice."* Here are some of the testimonies:

Testimony of Mr. Shingi Saigusa (lawyer):

"After Mass we went to dinner at the House of Saint Joseph where the men were staying. It was already late, perhaps 9:30. We were at table when a telephone call from the convent alerted us that the statue was crying again. Father Yasuda told us: 'She is crying at this moment. What shall we do?'

"Instinctively, everybody rose from the table to run to the chapel. Indeed the tears flowed from the eyes of the statue. As for me, who was the first to arrive, I wept with sobs in my voice. I was near the foot of the altar when the Rosary began, but I was unable to repress my tears which flowed without stopping. I believe that the statue shed more tears this day than the day before.

"After the prayer, we returned to the House of Saint Joseph to finish dinner, but no one spoke further and a great emotion reigned around the table."

Witness of Mr. Mitsuo Kawashima:

"The next day, a little after midday, we had sat down at table when the news came. We were then witnesses a second time. The tears of the night before had left traces on the face and new drops streamed on the cheeks."

Witness of Mr. Isao Suzuki:

"Having had a technical training, I have a tendency to learn everything by reasoning. I am of those who prefer natural explanations to supernatural phenomena. Also the first time that I saw the tears, I asked myself at once if it was not due to the rain which had humidified the wood. It was at the second lachrymation that I truly experienced a shock. There was no natural explanation possible."

Witness of Mr. Eiji Hiroi:

"When I heard the news, I also asked if it was not humidity because of the weather and when I understood that this could not be the case as I observed the phenomenon more closely, I thought of the possibility of some fakery with a syringe.

"However, the second time I clearly saw the tears flowing from the pupils and streaming one after the other. This time I could not remain insensible before a prodigy which surpassed all human comprehension."

Testimony of Mr. Saimon Miyata (university professor):

"The second time, I do not know how to describe what I felt at the sight of the drops which appeared in the corner of the eyes giving off beautiful luminous reflections before pearling on the cheek."

Witness of Mr. Kiyokazu Fujii:

"The first time, it was so unexpected that I remained stupefied. I had prayed the Rosary asking pardon for my sins, though I could not raise my eyes and looked simply at the tears streaming near the feet without looking in greater detail.

"The second time I observed attentively. Large drops formed beads which flowed from the left eye onto the cheek and I had the feeling of being face to face with a prodigy in which no human artifice was involved."

Witness of Mr. Tadao Moriguchi:

"I also was very impressed the first time and I could not observe the tears attentively, but I was not yet convinced that evening. When it had happened the next day I looked closely. It is not something which one can explain by invoking simply natural or psychic causes.

"Even for an atheist it is inadmissible to decree that what one does not understand cannot exist, and to deny apriori without asking questions about what one has seen with one's own eyes. I hope that what I saw (the supernatural force manifested before me) has served to increase my faith."

Witness of Mr. Yasuhiro Izaki (president of a company):

"Certainly I had reason to go to Akita, but in no way did I expect to see the tears of the Virgin. Evidently I was ready to believe in the miraculous events concerning the blood, the perspiration, the perfumes, but I did not have the least pretension, furthermore unthought of, to go to verify them myself.

"I indeed saw tears appear and accumulate at the corner of the eyes and flow silently along the cheeks. I immediately prostrated myself, forgetting the world around me. I had the very strong feeling that all of our little personal affairs and the desires related to them are futile and vain. Was it an inspiration of Heaven?

"God has hidden these things from the learned and the wise and has revealed them to little ones, the Bible teaches us. I am filled with fear at the thought that the All Powerful God has manifested Himself to us... to the nothingness that I am.

"Faith is not a *part* of an individual, and still less, an accessory. It must concern the entire personality, and all our actions. This is what I profoundly felt because of this experience."

Witness of Mr. Fumio Ono:

"After the first lachrymation I discussed it that evening with Mr. Hiroi, and we raised the possibility of fakery with a syringe. The second time, while trying to keep my *sang-froid* (I told myself, 'Don't become eccentric') I decided to look seriously.

"The tears formed and flowed without stopping. I approached very close to assure myself better. Then I understood that it was not something to doubt and I prayed the Rosary with the others."

Witness of Mr. Hiroshi Kawasaki:

"The second time, I approached within 30 centimeters (about one foot) from the statue and I saw tears large as a grain of rice come forth from the right eye and fall, throwing off reflections of light. It was of a beauty which human artifice, even though artistic, could not express. Had I been alone I would have been tempted to take the drops which had fallen to the foot of the statue and place them on my Rosary."

After citing the above testimony, the editor of *Catholic Graph* added: "The eleven witnesses have different attitudes. Some say that they will always repeat the same testimony without ever changing a word, and others are more reserved and think that one must speak of this with prudence, taking into account the dispositions of the person to whom we speak. But all are unanimous in saying one cannot deny the events of Yuzawadai nor take them lightly and that they require a loyal inquiry whose results ought to be made public as soon as possible."

As for myself, I had been witness of the lachrymations of the two days (except for the second because I had gone to the city) and I have already described what I saw. And since then I have often spoken of this to numerous visitors who came to pray at the convent.

It seems that the events of this day, the Feast of Saint Joseph and First Saturday, merit a more special attention as suggested by the words of the angel. The exhortation to "*Attach a greater importance to this day,*" appears like the assurance that the devotion to Saint Joseph pleases the Lord *(and to the importance of the First Saturdays).* Heaven wishes to encourage each one to bring this into daily life. But what stands out with particular importance in the words of the angel is the pressing invitation to put the messages of Our Lady into practice.

As we have remarked once before, could Heaven go to any greater lengths to attract our attention and impress us with the importance of this message manifested through tears and of urgent importance to each and every one of us?

✝✝✝

Chapter Fourteen

The Church and The Media

The 13th of May is a date when Catholics around the world commemorate the first apparition of Our Lady of Fatima. For this day, Pope John XXIII instituted the Liturgy of the "Feast of Our Lady of the Rosary of Fatima."

On the 13th of May of 1976, Mr. and Mrs. Keisuke Yama'uchi, journalist and editor of the *Catholic Graph*, were privileged witnesses to a lachrymation.

It was a year and a half before that the *Catholic Graph* had published a series of articles on "The Virgin of Akita." Other magazines and newspapers had reprinted the news, and two or three television networks had shown "The Statue Which Weeps" on the little screen. Thus the secular media drew attention of the public to such an extent that the Japanese Catholic press wanted to hear nothing more about it and fell into an obstinate silence on the subject.

For my part, I sent exact information to various Catholic centers of information but nothing was published. So I wrote to the *Catholic Graph*, offering to put all the documents at their disposal.

The at least astonishing news of the lachrymations of the Virgin temporarily increased the circulation of the magazine, but at the same time drew upon it the anger of people who were apriori opposed. Mr. Yama'uchi often told me of his concern for the future of his work, "Since we speak of the Virgin of Akita, the very existence of our review is in danger."

Now on this 13th of May, 1976, Mr. Yama'uchi had the providential opportunity to assist himself at a lachrymation. The article in which he relates his experience begins by telling of the difficulties he met in making known the events of Akita. Opposition from within the Church was so great that he confesses that he did not know how he could continue because of his feeble resources. He added, "This work became, for me above all, an insupportable burden..."

On this 13th of May when he came to the convent, Mr. Yama'uchi had already prepared the next issue of *Catholic*

Graph in which he was going to publish the interviews of the eleven witnesses of the lachrymations of the first and second of May (the first of May was not only the Feast of Saint Joseph the Worker, but also the First Saturday of the Month). Now less than two weeks later, having taken the decision to publish these testimonies, he relates the state of despondency which he felt when he arrived at Akita. He confided to us the bitter complaint he addressed to Mary as he prostrated before Her statue:

"I put myself out to try to bring to life a Catholic journal in the service of loyal and honest information, but the result is that I am at the end of my strength. I can do no more. I believe that it is thanks to Your miraculous help that we have been able to avoid failure to the present day. I thank Your Grace for that... but the collective interview which I am preparing to publish will finally do nothing but repeat that such and such a one has seen this and that. Then, if these facts are authentic, give me the grace to be among the witnesses. Would I not have much more to say with much more credibility? But it is You that will decide and not I. May it be done according to Your will. But as for me, I can do no more."

The Divine Response

Mr. and Mrs. Yama'uchi took the train from Tokyo the night before and they arrived in Yuzawadai in the morning after breakfast and Eucharistic adoration.

Briefly these are the circumstances which brought Mr. Yama'uchi to witness the tears of Mary. First his wife had pointed to the holy water font at the entrance to the chapel. "It has a fragrance," she said. "Not especially," he answered. Then she wet her finger and made the Sign of the Cross several times. "It is true, more now," she added.

That afternoon both of them went to the chapel which seemed empty. Looking at the statue to the right of the altar, Mr. Yama'uchi saw not only the face but the *entire body giving off a white light.* Remembering that the statue had been dark when he saw it in the morning, he called his wife and went closer: "I came as close as 30 centimeters, no... 10 centimeters, to observe.

"A drop of water shone on the end of the nose. Large round drops had stopped on the right cheek. The right eye was wet and shooting off reflections, and from the lower lid began the trace of a thread of water developing into drops. Drawing back I exclaimed: 'She weeps!' My wife sat down, saying that she was afraid. My eyes did not leave the statue and all sorts of thoughts filled my mind."

Gathering himself together, Mr. Yama'uchi wanted to recite a Hail Mary, but his voice was too broken with emotion and he could not. When he began to pray more slowly, his wife began to cry with great sobs. (She recounts that she prayed for the first time in her life with a truly childlike heart and that she felt the presence of God very close to her at that moment.) Shortly after, Mr. Yama'uchi hastened to find me in my office and I at once followed him to the chapel.

On that day twenty parishioners of Akita had come to participate in a Day of Recollection. At the announcement of the news they all assembled in the chapel and we were witnesses of the phenomenon. As in the preceding times I led the Rosary. When it was over, the areas wet with tears retained a reddish color clearly visible. Mr. Yama'uchi describes the condition of the statue in his article:

"When we were coming to the end of the Rosary, the water which had accumulated at the neck disappeared from our eyes in the space of an instant. *They disappear, they disappear*, I said to myself looking at this strange phenomenon which unfolded before me as in a film. From the place where I was I cannot verify what happened to the tears on the cheek and on the chin, but I very well observed the change which took place at the level of the neck."

When the phenomenon was over, he felt that it was the response of God to his prayer and at the same time an encouragement to continue to publish the review no matter what it cost. It is thus that the *Catholic Graph* continued to appear for many years.

Growing Trials

Opposition and criticism flowed from all sides as the Catholic Graph informed the public about the weeping of the statue of Akita, giving the miracle the importance which it deserved.

Bishop Ito, the highest religious person responsible with regard to these events, was not one to simply observe the situation in a passive way. One year before, he had asked a priest who was well known for research in Mariology to cooperate in an inquiry. This priest came in person to Yuzawadai where he had interviews with the sisters and asked Sister Agnes, whom he had been observing, to lend him her intimate journal. He said that the articles that I had furnished until that time did not permit objective judgment because they presented everything in a favorable light without any allusion to what might be negative.

After a moment of reflection, I told Sister Agnes that she could give him the journal, judging that it was not proper to withhold anything whatever if that could be useful for discerning the truth.

It was a year later that the intimate journal was returned and in reality had been used to show that the sister was a psychopath using "ectoplasmic" powers! This marked the beginning of a most sorrowful period not only for Sister Agnes but for all of us. It was only eight years later that the accusation would fall with the publication of the pastoral letter of the Bishop after much more detailed inquiries.

TRANSLATOR'S NOTE:

At this point in his book, Father Yasuda speaks at some length of the terrible trial which ensued not for just days or weeks, but for several years. While it fills only a few pages, certainly all the encouragement of Our Lady and of the angel were necessary to come through this terrible time. One is put in mind of the sufferings of Lucia after the apparitions of Fatima, when she was repeatedly taken to the priest by her mother and told to confess that she had lied, even to the point of having been beaten several times and accused of leading her entire family to disgrace and ruin.

Four days after the visit of Mr. and Mrs. Yama'uchi, this same priest (whom we shall call the inquisitor) came to preach a week's retreat. Bishop Ito agreed with this because he had asked this priest to cooperate in that inquiry and he thought that his meeting with the community would facilitate the task. As for me, I had been invited to go to speak at a church in Suzuka, of the prefecture of Miea, and I took advantage to do this during the time of the retreat.

Without doubt by an effect of Divine Providence, Sister Agnes was called to the bedside of her dying mother in her native village and had to leave the convent the first day of the retreat. And thus the inquisitor had an open field to give free course to his verve for a whole week.

When I returned from the trip I was surprised by the leaden silence and the heavy atmosphere which reigned among the sisters. Several days passed and the following Sunday they came to find me in my office after breakfast. They began by explaining that the inquisitor had caused them to doubt everything. They had been obliged to agree that they had no argument to oppose his coherent and structured demonstration, according to which everything was a result of ectoplasmic powers of Sister Agnes who had to be a psychopath and, everything considered, there was no other solution than to take the side of the inquisitor.

For the moment I protested vigorously "What idiocy!" but I soon realized that it was fruitless to try to deny a theory based on a third person report. I had to meet the inquisitor in person to understand his so convincing arguments.

As I reflect upon it, there was nothing surprising in the fact that the first conviction of the sisters was overcome before the large-worded interpretations of a theologian strong in Marian questions. It was a total impasse and I was deeply disturbed. Even the trees and the flowers of the Garden of Mary no longer brought joy to my heart. Everything seemed covered with a gray veil which seemed to block out any prospect of solution. I had doleful states of soul when I thought how fragile can be our human convictions.

So two days later I went to see the inquisitor in Tokyo with two superiors of the convent. We were received in the parlor of the Institute of Theology for an interview which lasted two hours. The inquisitor gave us the explanations which follow, citing his detailed inquiry in which he sifted the intimate journal of Sister Agnes.

His study revealed that since Sister Agnes was a psychopath from birth she had already manifested ectoplasmic powers before being converted to Christianity and that these powers had resurfaced after her conversion. The wound which appeared on the hand of the statue, the blood which flowed, the phenomena of perspiration and lachrymation, all could be explained by this so called ectoplasm which she had, that is to say that she was able to transfer her own blood upon the hand of the statue, and the same with the tears.

He had an air of certainty of what he said and cited as support the occult practices of certain Buddhist sects. When he was finished speaking, I said to myself that the object of my research would have to now bear on the question of knowing what precise relation of cause and effect existed between the so-called powers of the sister and the objective phenomena we witnessed on the statue. The theory of this renowned theologian satisfied me not at all.

For his part, bearing the primary responsibility in the Church, Bishop Ito began to feel the urgency of concrete action and decided to ask the advice of the Apostolic Nuncio. The latter suggested that he ask the Archbishop of Tokyo for the creation of the commission of canonical inquiry without delay, so a commission was officially created, and the inquisitor, whose position was already well known, was named president. On the order of the commission, Bishop Ito made an official declaration in the *Catholic Journal*, official press organ of the Japanese Church, forbidding all public manifestation of veneration towards the statue of the Virgin of Akita.

At the same time Sister Agnes was called by the inquisitor to answer to a long interrogation. It lasted an entire day during which she was forced to hear argument upon argument, undergoing a true brainwashing. The inquisitor had already explained, over and over and to numerous personalities from different areas, what he thought of Sister Agnes, calling her a "special psychopathic case" characterized by a disassociation, the visions which she said to have seen of the guardian angel being only a manifestation of her double personality of which she herself was the dupe. And he added that her spiritual director used her for writing articles in the media and accumulating benefices, which was an inadmissible sin.

But this did not prevent him from welcoming Sister Agnes with open arms, without a single word of reproach and even with a strong mark of affection worthy of a father. Was it to gain her favor? Sister Agnes relates: "When I arrived, accompanied by my brother and my sister, he (the inquisitor) welcomed us with open arms and a warm smile. We were very moved by his very paternal kindness. He had had a very nice breakfast prepared for us.

"Then we found ourselves alone, face to face, and I had to listen to the development of his arguments from morning until 5 o'clock in the afternoon, without the time to breathe.

"I saw coming the moment when I was going to be squarely labeled mentally ill, but this word was not pronounced a single time. It was when he declared that I had ectoplasmic powers that I began seriously to be disturbed. To my question as to what he meant by that, he explained at length that that came from the subconscious, and so on and that all the mysterious phenomena were due to my subconscious action.

"'Then that comes from the devil? In these conditions, I pray you to drive them from me.' 'It is not the devil. There is no fault on your part because it is subconscious.'

"'But I cannot be a victim of this monstrosity. And since you say that I abuse very many people in this way, it is a frightening thing. I beg you, free me from these powers.'

"'In any event it is not you who are at fault. One can say that the responsibility falls on your superior who took this story of the angel seriously from the beginning and that let this snowball. The words of the angel, it is you who recount them to yourself.' He exhorted me to pay no more attention to these apparitions.

"However, the guardian angel appeared to me during the Mass at 11 o'clock which followed although I did not expect her there. I hastily closed my eyes not to pay attention but I immediately heard her voice which said, *'Do not fear,'* and from that I had a feeling of indescribable peace.

"At the beginning of the afternoon interview, I explained that the angel had come again and he told me that this was altogether normal because that could not stop all of a sudden since the time I had had these visions, but that everything would soon return to order because he was there to direct me... and the sermon began in the same style...

"The thing which upset me the most in what he said, even supposing that I was not at fault, was that I was abusing a great number of people. At the end, I felt myself completely battered down and my sister, advised by telephone, came to get me with a taxi. In the taxi I was asking myself if I would come out of this alive, emptied as I was of all energy.

"I did not want even to look at the dinner which my sister had prepared for me with such solicitude and taking my head in my hands, my face resting on the table, I jumped when I felt a strange sensation on my fingers. My hair had literally stood up on my head, without doubt because of fear; it was completely stiffened by grease and sweat as though someone had planted stiff needles which my fingers could not penetrate.

"After a frightened instant, I took hold of myself suddenly as if waking from a sleep. 'What are you about? And you imagine that you have the faith? Nothing happens without permission of God, and does not He know it all? Is it not to be the victim of oneself, tormenting the soul like that?' This light suddenly freed me and I almost felt like laughing because the situation was truly funny. When I lifted up my hands again in the midst of a laugh wet with tears, my hair had regained its suppleness.

"The next day, thanks to the good care of Bishop Ito, I was hospitalized for a complete examination of my physical and psychic state. I stretched out on the bed at the end of my strength. For three days the doctors kept going and coming, and I was unable either to eat or to raise myself. Three weeks later, two Sisters took me to a thermal station for a period of convalescence.

"When I returned to the convent after having regained my strength, I found there an ambiance completely different from what it had been before. From this day on I had the impression of living, walking on needles. When I think of it now I wonder how I ever survived alive. At the moment of hospitalization, I was in a state of extreme moral and physical exhaustion. I said to myself more than once that I would indeed be happier if the good God would call me to Himself at once!"

One must realize that this account rather minimizes the reality, the memories being strongly diminished with the passage of the years after that shock of "spiritual direction."

In appearance the people were gentle. The doctors at the hospital never spoke to her openly about mental illness themselves and persistently told her that she was normal, while in the report sent to the canonical commission they refer to a specific case of hysteria.

At the convent, the superior and the other sisters treated her kindly, but she knew too well that her credibility was reduced to nothing and she was considered with doubt in all that she did. She confided to me later that she clung with all her strength to the words that I whispered to her, "Christ on the Cross was rejected and abandoned by all."

Thus for her began long days of trial and moral solitude in the midst of general misunderstanding.

Thermal Cure

Sister Agnes had always been of fragile health from her infancy. It was not rare that she would go several times a year for a thermal cure. Professor Okuhara now counseled this treatment for her at the thermal baths of Y. She there found a haven of warm peace of which she had so much need in order to recover from the sad trials she had had to undergo.

In that isolated village in the hollow of the mountains, a place so familiar to her, she found the attentive welcome of the director of the establishment to which was added the beneficial effect of the warm waters. Nevertheless, the absence of daily Mass and of the Eucharist must have been extremely difficult to bear for a person desiring and devoting her life in prayer in a convent.

Bishop Ito was able to make only three short visits of a day during the three months she was there. As for myself, I could hardly do more than bring her Communion one or two times a month, covering the 170 kilometers by train or bus. I spoke to her of the Passion of Our Lord and I enjoined her to draw courage from it. She answered that she felt sustained by this meditation.

When she said "Stripped of all her energies" she was also making reference to other events which affected her deeply. Indeed, some will say that there was not sufficient reason to be put into such a state by a single day of "brainwashing" but we must remember that Sister Agnes' health was just sufficient to lead the community life of the convent at the same tempo of the others. Moreover, *she had just lost her mother.* And at the beginning of *the same year,* she had been affected by *the death of her father* whom she so much loved. Now her mother left her... this mother whom she had caused so much fatigue and worry, with her fragile health, her long malady, her eleven operations and the Last Sacraments administered twice when she was at the point of death. The profound sorrow that she felt because of this weighed heavily on her fragile shoulders.

And it was *precisely in these difficult moments* that they came to take her literally by force to Tokyo (her family obviously opposed it) in order to submit to the "good offices" of the inquisitor. To all this must be added the fact that *she was completely deaf!*... something those around her had a tendency to forget. And total deafness does not seem to be simply a handicap as one would be tempted to think. Just imagine the anguish into which a person is plunged who hears nothing. Dangers can strike from behind, impossible to avoid. She did succeed well in communicating normally thanks to lip reading and an innate intuition, but her nerves must have been perpetually strained.

Hardly had she been presented to the inquisitor than she had to follow a sermon which didn't finish. And this in a very proper Japanese, requiring a particularly sustained attention necessary to read the lips of a stranger. The sermon consisted of showing the abuse people made of the use of ectoplasmic faculties. And for someone who finds her joy and reason for living in the service of God and of others, this brutal shock took a terrible toll of her physical and moral resistance. So now perhaps one can comprehend the state of extreme exhaustion after the fear which had actually caused her hair to stand straight on her head.

Then the three weeks in the hospital were an uninterrupted succession of medical examinations. *She had no rest whatever.* When she could finally leave, she had been *injured in the shock of an abrupt landing of the plane and had to be transported in a wheelchair!* In brief, each day brought its share of trials so that it is no wonder, from just the brief overview that I have given above, we can understand how she wondered if she would live through it all.

Happily a convalescence at the thermal station of Y. was most beneficial. When I went to see her she let me know that she did not feel any solitude, sustained by meditation on the Passion. Furthermore, she did not have the air of being depressed. Loving person that she was, Sister Agnes very soon had bonds of friendship with the family of the establishment and the others taking the cure.

She explains that her greatest pleasure was in the company of the birds of the mountain. They came one after the other to pick the crumbs of cake which she spread at the edge of the window. They ate from her hand. They rested on her arms, her shoulders, and even her head. Even the most timid birds came to see her to the joy of all around. Furthermore, the visits of "the guardian angel" continued contrary to the affirmation of the inquisitor, "She will not appear more." The angel appeared often at Sister's side, encouraging her with a sweet smile and sometimes saying the Rosary with her.

Three months passed in this way, and with the fresh breezes of autumn she had sufficiently recovered her strength to return to the convent.

The Plans of Providence

As we have already seen, the atmosphere which awaited Sister Agnes when she returned to the convent was not at all the same as before. Her companions were troubled not knowing what attitude to adopt now that the mysterious events which had so much overwhelmed them were relegated to the cupboard of ectoplasms. It must have been quite difficult for them to show the same attention to her now denounced by the authority as "the instigatrix" of the affair.

For my part, I continued to speak of the events in the monthly bulletin of the community, furnishing new information connected with it. At the same time, I suggested to the community to discreetly meditate on these things with humility as signs sent by the Lord.

However, after I published the detailed account of the lachrymation of the first of May, Bishop Ito sent me this order: "This kind of information risks provoking misunderstandings. Since a commission of inquiry has been charged to study the matter, keep silence until the conclusions are published."

From that time on, I no longer spoke for a certain time, keeping myself to diverse events of the life of the convent. Nevertheless it would happen that I would briefly recall this or that special fact. Thus a Korean woman of advanced age had, during a stay at Yuzawadai, experienced a sweet perfume emanating from the statue, something which had not happened for a long time. She said that the events of Yuzawadai were widely known in Korea through a book entitled *The Virgin Mary Weeps at Akita* (already 20 thousand copies sold, exhausting the edition), and that the Catholics of Korea believed in the truth of the miracle and dreamed of coming here in pilgrimage.

Now the phenomena of the tears had stopped completely from the moment when the commission of inquiry was begun. And I concluded at that time that they were definitely terminated.

Two years later, this commission decided not to recognize the supernatural character of the events. But no details were given to us on the content of the study. Bishop Ito commanded that we submit to the conclusions of the commission without discussion after they were published. One of the sisters asked if it was necessary to obey even when conscience opposed. He had confirmed, "In a case like this, it is important to obey."

However, it would seem that Bishop Ito was very troubled by the negative conclusion of the commission and he was not able to decide to make a public declaration on the subject. Instead, some months later he went personally to Rome to the Congregation for the Doctrine of the Faith, and the Congregation for the Propagation of the Faith. There he exposed all the facts and asked the advice of authorized persons. He was given the following advice: "If you are not convinced by the conclusions of this commission, you must form another yourself and begin the study from the beginning."

As we have already seen, the intimate journal of Sister Agnes had been photocopied and used by the inquisitor as the unique piece of the dossier with the intention of denying everything. *And the judgment was pronounced without any member of the said commission,* outside of the inquisitor, *ever having put foot in the convent of Yuzawadai* to verify the facts, to live the daily life of the convent, and to better know the dispositions and spirit of the members. To base such an important decision solely on the intimate journal without finding the need to come and find out for oneself is indeed a curious way of fulfilling such a grave responsibility.

When the second commission was created on the initiative of the Bishop, the result of the first was known by all. For my part, the more I studied what had happened, the more evident to me it was that the events were supernatural.

Throughout the inquiries, the life of the convent continued without any particular change. And by little groups, pilgrims continued to come from the four corners of the country.

U.S. Pilgrims with Sister Agnes and members of the community.

Chapter Fifteen

New Signs

As we have seen, we had asked the aid of Saint Joseph in order that we might complete the Garden of Mary. Having learned the request of the angel, "It is sad that there is no exterior sign here in honor of Saint Joseph. Ask your superior to have an exterior sign erected in his honor when you are able, even if it is not right away," I hastened to acquire a little statue of Saint Joseph which I had placed in such a way as to make it a counterpart to that of Mary, at the other side of the altar.

Shortly afterwards, M. H., who frequented our prayer meetings, expressed a desire to offer a statue of the saint in wood which he ordered from M. Saburo Wakasa, sculptor of the statue of the Virgin. The statue was delivered six months later. It was made in such a way as to accord very well with that of the Virgin, of the same height and from the same wood. Meanwhile, because of the inquiry, the statue of Our Lady had been removed to the corner, and so we decided to place the statue of Saint Joseph there beside that of Our Lady on the 15th of August, the solemn day we had chosen for its blessing.

At the beginning of July, we were visited by 32 children from the prefecture of Wakayama, accompanied by Mr. and Mrs. Y., directors of a private school. These youths of elementary school and of college had not been baptized and I was wondering what we could do that might leave with them a good memory of the long trip that they had made to Akita.

To celebrate the second anniversary of the Garden and at the same time to thank Saint Joseph to whom it owed its existence, I had the idea of a procession in the Garden carrying the holy patron at the head of the cortege. I spoke of this to Mr. and Mrs. Y. and to the sisters and all agreed. Such a manifestation might appear childish at first sight, but any act of faith implies a childish candor and this one seemed to me quite proper for the young people. Thus on the evening of the 26th of July, the day of their arrival, we processed around the Garden several times, the boys at the head with the statue of Saint Joseph on their shoulders as though preparing for the blessing which was to take place some days later. The adults followed with candles, singing hymns between decades of the Rosary. It was a very beautiful procession.

After the procession, which lasted about an hour, we brought the statue of Saint Joseph back into the room to be placed next to the statue of Mary. And hardly had the sacristy sister put on the light than she exclaimed: "The statue of the Virgin weeps again!"

At first I thought she was joking, but she signaled for me to come while I was still at the doorway. It was true, streams of completely fresh tears were visible from the chin down to the neckpiece. Evidently, it was a question of the very same phenomenon of weeping which had stopped two years earlier and which had been repeated ten times.

At the announcement of the news, more than 50 persons, including the children, gathered in the little room. Among them were Mr. and Mrs. H., donors of the statue of Saint Joseph. They had come especially that day to participate in the candlelight procession. By the end of the second decade of the Rosary, the tears were completely dried.

For the children it was a memorable pilgrimage in the distant region of Michinoku, in the midst of the candles, the songs and the prayers. And they carried in their hearts the candid joy of being the knights of Saint Joseph. They had contemplated the tears with astonishment. For them, Mary expressed Her joy in seeing them gathered about Her; they were full of warmth and happiness when it came time to leave.

Without doubt Mr. H. also saw in the tears of Mary a sign of thanksgiving for the donation of Saint Joseph. Unfortunately it was not possible to ask his impressions because he died suddenly the following day. His spouse relates that during a game of golf he had been suddenly surprised by a violent pain in his neck. He soon succumbed to a heart attack. The evening before when they were going to return by car after the festivities in the Garden of Mary, he had proposed to his wife to come to pray at Yuzawadai every day. Greatly absorbed in his work as an inventor, he had never shown very fervent faith. He was baptized before he died, and he must have been profoundly impressed by the tears of Mary to have taken such a resolution. His wife had the consolation of seeing him called to God in excellent disposition of soul.

Having announced that the lachrymations would not last a long time, the inquisitor found it perfectly normal that they had not recurred in two years after the inquiry had begun. This is what he had affirmed to me when I visited him in person to know exactly his point of view and his arguments. According to him, his theological investigations had revealed that the sister had voluntarily provoked the tenth lachrymation just before the beginning of the inquiry in order to influence the judgment.

Nevertheless, Our Lady, through the statue, had as it were guarded silence for two years and two months, relegated to an antichamber, and now began to weep absolutely as if She had waited until the unfavorable decision of the commission was known. It was the evening of the 26th of July, 1978. And after that the phenomenon would be repeated many times until the Feast of Our Lady of the Seven Sorrows.

TRANSLATOR'S NOTE:

Father Yasuda refers to his own suffering during these terrible two years in just one sentence, saying that there were times that he felt so "low" that he was tempted to give it all up. And he hardly spoke at much greater length about the terrible sufferings of Sister Agnes, which were so great that she wondered if she could possibly live through them. And what about the sufferings of the entire community? There was so much in that question put to the Bishop by just one of the sisters, "And if it is against our conscience, are we not to believe?"

And while the tears of Our Lady had always aroused great compassion and sorrow in them, causing them to weep, now after two years and two months the tears of Our Lady this time seemed like tears of joy. Father Yasuda remarks that the young children who witnessed this left with a feeling of warmth and happiness...undoubtedly reflecting his own joy after such a long, almost interminable period of trial, indeed a trial which he thought would not end because he had never expected that the statue would weep again, after two years of nothing but contradiction and crosses. And now a new inquiry had been set up by the Bishop which would certainly be influenced by the one conducted by the inquisitor who had stated flatly that the last lachrymation was deliberately brought on by Sister Agnes, and that there would be no more.

But Bishop Ito had gone to Rome for advice, and on that advice he had established a new inquiry. And at this dramatic moment Our Lady intervened by renewing the miracle.

From the beginning of the phenomenon of the tears on the 4th of January, 1975, until the Feast of Our Lady of Sorrows on the 15th of September, 1981, the statue has cried 101 times. A little later Bishop Ito had gone to the inquisitor to ask him what explanation he would give to the fact that the statue wept even when Sister Agnes was far from the convent. He obtained an answer, which to say the least, is surprising: "It is because another sister near the statue also possesses ectoplasmic faculties!"

I spoke above of the reaction of M. H. and his wife and of the children. For my part it was with renewed emotion that I saw the phenomenon of lachrymation again. Over and against the wisdom of humans who obstinately deny, God continues His work in Sovereign liberty. At least this is what I had felt in my interior conscience. And in fact, as to fill the void of those two years and two months, the statue of Our Lady now began to weep when She wished, as She wished. The thesis of tears caused by ectoplasm, accentuated by the announcement of the inquisitor that these mysterious events would soon cease, fell apart like a house of cards.

The value of a simple faith was taught to us here once again. One feels a necessity of reviving in our contemporary world, without seeking to minimize its sense, the teaching of Jesus, "If you have a faith as great as a mustard seed, you will say to that mountain to throw itself into the sea, and it will throw itself into the sea." *Each time that I saw the brown cheeks of the statue become wet as those of a living person, I could not fail to invoke Mary at the foot of the Cross by Her agonizing Son.*

More than any other artistic representation of the Passion, no matter how beautiful and well made, the sight of true human tears coming forth from a simple wooden statue has something so poignant that it touches directly to the heart. Nature is so made that even the most marked events, even those one should never forget, do not resist the usage of time; impressions tarnish and memories fade. In this regard, it seems to me that the tears of Our Lady are also a grace given to our time in order to revive in us the reminder of Christ suspended on the Cross, and of the sorrowful participation of Mary in His Divine Sacrifice.

The Memorable Days

If the weeping of the statue took place 101 times, it was never the same. As for the quantity, they could flow without stopping in abundance, or they might be reduced to two or three tears. Besides, from this time on the phenomenon rarely happened when the community was alone in the convent; more often it happened when there were visitors, that is in the presence of witnesses from outside whose observation would be more difficult to consider subjective. Moreover, the moment when the tears would flow was never fixed; they could appear in the middle of the day or during the night, without anyone being able to know in advance.

There was always someone to notice the tears, whether adults, children, visitors or sisters, without any distinction of persons. If one seeks a time when the tears never did occur, perhaps the only exception was the Holy Mass. The Mass is the most sacred liturgical act, central and indispensable in the life of the community. I remember that the tears flowed two or three times a little before or after Mass, but otherwise always at different times of the day or night.

At the end of this book we will give a chronological chart of the 101 lachrymations. But perhaps it is fitting here to recount just some of the more special examples.

Twenty-fifth of March, 1979

On March 25, 1979, tears flowed from the eyes of Mary after breakfast, just before the Eucharistic adoration. These were true streams of tears which covered Her face. We never saw them so abundant as at that time. On photos taken at the end of the phenomenon, one still clearly sees the traces. I recall that we interpreted these tears as a sign from Heaven in honor of the Annunciation, the feast of that day.

The tears flowed abundantly in the following period and even sometimes several days in a row during the months of May and June. On the last day of July the statue wept for the 95th time. In this period, the members of the community began to sort of take it for granted. We united to say the Rosary in a more distracted way, as if the phenomenon could be seen any old time. Some of the sisters even showed a certain lassitude when told that the statue was crying again while they were absorbed in their work. No one was sheltered from this human tendency to make little of something, over a long period, even though it ought to be taken most seriously. Then after the 31 of July the phenomenon abruptly stopped.

At the approach of autumn, after the heavy heat of summer, pilgrims came to render homage to the miraculous Virgin in ever greater numbers, but none of them could see the tears. Then came winter. Not a single tear flowed from the statue. What did the silence mean? Was it an interruption or was it the end? I was indeed troubled to find an answer.

Towards the end of the year I received a telephone call which to say the least was surprising. It was M. T., director of a television station. He said that he had received a bizarre telephone call from an anonymous person advising him above all not to speak of the "Tears of the Virgin of Akita." M. T. had never heard speak of the tears and this brief exchange peaked his curiosity. He had called M. Yama'uchi of the *Catholic Graph* to ask for more details. After that he wanted to come in person to learn about it and requested an interview. I was not very happy about furnishing information to the media, but since he said he wanted to know the truth I could not refuse.

Four persons from this television station arrived on the 6th of December, led by Mr. Yama'uchi. They were two days later than originally expected, bringing us closer to the Feast of the Immaculate Conception. As we shall see it proved to be a providential delay.

The 6th fell on Thursday evening before the First Friday of the month which is always preceded in our convent by a night of adoration with sisters taking turns before the Blessed Sacrament.

The statue of Our Lady was still in the parlor, next to the chapel, because the second board of inquiry was at work and the matter would still be under ecclesiastical examination until that commission had made its decision one way or the other, after which the Bishop would make a pronouncement.

The technicians had brought their material and set up a camera before the statue, regulating it in such a way that it would snap a picture every six seconds. And although it was in a room separate from the chapel, the noise of the automatic camera release resounded in the silence of the night. So I decided to postpone the adoration to the following night. Besides, now the night adoration would be a preparation for the Feast of the Immaculate Conception the day following. So to say the camera monopolized the statue until the beginning of Mass the following morning, implacably repeating the same operation hour after hour, but it photographed nothing unusual.

The next day, December 7th, we were requisitioned for an interview, and then a tour of the garden etc., and our visitors thus used up our time until evening. As night fell, they rested their tired bodies, and we began the night adoration which had been transferred from the day before.

On the 8th of December, a little after midnight, more precisely at ten minutes after, the telephone rang in my room. The statue had been discovered in tears. I at once called Mr. Yama'uchi and his technicians who were sleeping on the first floor and making sure that they had understood me, I ran to the convent.

I had hardly arrived at the statue before the technicians, who had followed close behind, bombarded the statue with their cameras and photographic apparatus. I had to admire the promptitude and dexterity of these picture specialists. Some later said that the first pictures were spoiled because their hands trembled. As usual, we recited the Rosary with the pilgrims present and with our own eyes saw the end of the lachrymation.

In the morning the camera men asked to remain another day, regretting not having placed the camera the previous evening as they had on the day they arrived. They wanted to try a second time. It was a legitimate request and I had no objection. So the camera was replaced on the evening of the 8th of December about 8 o'clock and the lapse set to snap at regular intervals.

It was past 11 o'clock when one of the sisters, kneeling before the statue after a final visit to the Blessed Sacrament, discovered the tears again. Later, the film taken that evening was shown on television throughout all of Japan in a course of a program which proposed to answer the question, *lie or reality?*

Today this videotape is shown all over the world, and we show it to the pilgrims who come to the convent, if they desire to see it, and thus as we were nearing the very end of this prolonged miracle, it was prolonged in such a way that many, many thousands all over the world have also become witnesses.

One can only render thanks to the Providence which awaited the Feast of the Immaculate Conception to manifest this prodigy in such a way that it is preserved for the sight of many.

Decisive Expertise

The feast of August 22nd, 1981, Feast of the Queen of the World, was in the old calendar the Feast of the Immaculate Heart of Mary. There is nothing in particular about the tears which the statue shed that day, but it is fitting that we recall them in order that we may better understand what is to follow.

The first scientific analysis which I had requested concerning the tears of January 4th 1975, had revealed that it was a question of human liquid. However, the presence of "human liquids" foreign to the statue had created a problem with regard to the ongoing inquiry; it had provoked doubts of some and had poisoned the argument. I therefore was looking for an occasion to gather the liquids with extreme care to avoid all impurity. On that day I took immense precautions. Taking a new morsel of cotton with tweezers, I made a ball about as large as an apricot seed, then I carried it beneath the wooden chin where a drop was clinging and after having absorbed it in the cotton, I put it into a sack of new vinyl.

The afternoon of the same day I took it to the University of Akita. The analysis was requested from Professor Sagisaka of the faculty of Legal Medicine of the University of Gifu, on the recommendation of Professor Okuhara of the number one laboratory of biochemistry of Akita.

Professor Sagisaka, loaded with work, sent me the results only three months later, through the hands of Professor Okuhara in the form of the very complete certificate containing nine articles:

1. Name of the person asking for the analysis.
2. Day of the request.
3. Object to be analyzed
4. Content of the analysis.
5. Tests with antihuman rabbit serum
6. Analysis of blood group.
7. Explanation.
8. Analysis of blood group.
9. Result of analysis, which was given in the following words: "The object examined has adhering to it *human liquids* which *belong to the blood group O.*

"Made by the faculty of Legal Medicine of the University of Gifu, the 30th of November, 1981. Expert: Karou Sagisaka."

This expert analysis is the only authentic scientific proof which we have kept with regard to the tears of the statue. It played a decisive role in the recognition of the facts.

As we have already seen over and over, the phenomenon had been attributed by the first commission to the ectoplasmic faculties of Sister Agnes. She had firmly declared that she had no knowledge of such powers, but was told that this was something from her subconscious, thus cutting short all objection.

The blood group revealed by the scientific analysis was a determining factor. Sister Agnes belongs to group B. The first analysis had established that the blood which appeared on the wound of the right hand of the statue was of group B. As for the tears which flowed from the eyes, they belonged to a person of group AB, always according to the first expert analysis. As we indicated before, the inquisitor had ignored that the tears were of group AB at that time when he insisted on the ectoplasmic theory. And now on the examination taken later, without any adherence of impurities, revealed that they belong to group O.

As one compares the first expert analysis and the second, it is established that the blood and the tears coming from the statue belong to three different blood groups. How could a human being fabricate two blood groups to which he did not belong? Is not the pure act of creation the privilege of God?

God has manifested here His creative force. He first created the blood of group B, then the perspiration and the tears of group AB and finally of group O, as though to place an *absolute and final refutation* to the senseless thesis of paranormal powers invented by the detractors.

I sometimes wonder if it had not been for this second expert analysis (with the irrefutable scientific proof) whether the thesis of ectoplasm might not have continued its ravages, drowning all in an erroneous interpretation of the facts and abusing souls of good will who seek only to render homage to the supernatural action of God.

The Second Commission — Positive Ruling

On September 12, 1981, the second commission of inquiry, formed at the request of Bishop Ito, held its last session. At the time of the meeting which took place in May, Bishop Ito read a provisional report, written in his own hand, in which he asked for recognition of the facts. No members of the commission were openly opposed, but all decision was put off for the last meeting. In the interval, Bishop Ito received a letter from the Holy See advising him to be careful. This warning had certainly been inspired by the negative conclusion of the first commission.

When the second commission was concluded, four members voted in favor of recognizing the events as supernatural, and three did not. Despite the favorable majority, Bishop Ito preferred to abstain from any official declaration authenticating the supernaturality of the events in order to remain faithful to the attitude of prudence counseled by Rome.

On the morning of this same day, the statue of the Virgin wept for the one hundredth time.

The sisters telephoned to Niigata in order that the members of the commission might be informed before their meeting. The response was, "We cannot consider the tears of the statue as a determining sign or a miracle. The supernaturality of the facts can only be recognized *if more important miracles take place.*"

There had been one hundred lachrymations and that was still not enough. The more weak the faith, the more one requires spectacular signs. However, it is impossible to recognize the supernatural nature of a fact, whatever it be, without the light of faith. The numerous miracles operated by Christ were denied purely and simply by those of the Jews who were incredulous by their disposition of spirit. It is therefore not surprising that a hundred lachrymations of the statue of the Mother of Christ did not yet suffice in order that one judge it enough.

In the beginning the inquisitor, leader of the opposition, had himself declared, "One or two tears do not suffice. They can be evoked by ectoplasmic faculties of someone. When the quantity will be sufficiently abundant in order that such faculties cannot be invoked, in that condition it would be convenient to believe that that comes from Heaven." However, even when the statue had wept abundantly (it happened that the tears accumulated in the folds of the garment and fell even down to the globe), those who did not wish to believe did not. The fact that a person believes or doesn't believe in the supernatural, does not relate to the more or less spectacular character of the matter, but to the disposition of the person to believe or not believe in Divine intervention in our world. In other terms, acceptance comes by faith and faith alone.

A little later the guardian angel said to Sister Agnes, *"They ask a miracle greater than the tears; there will be no more."**

---

*There were to be further miracles, but the miracle of tears was to cease.

The Last Weeping — Our Lady of Sorrows

On the Feast of Our Lady of Sorrows, September 15th, 1981, the statue again shed tears about 2 o'clock in the afternoon. Sixty-five persons were present: a group of parishioners of Akita, visitors from more distant regions and some sisters of the motherhouse of the Institute. The quantity of tears was moderate. Nevertheless the witnesses were very moved by the fact that it happened exactly on the day of the Feast of Our Lady of Sorrows. From the words of the angel I didn't have the slightest doubt that these would be the last tears shed by Our Lady at Yuzawadai. It was the one hundred and first time that She wept. It is not a round figure and *aside from the words of the angel,* there was nothing to cause us to think that it was the end of the lachrymations.

Two weeks later, the 28th of September, Sister Agnes suddenly felt the presence of the angel at her side during the adoration of the Blessed Sacrament. She did not see the angel in person but a Bible appeared open before her eyes and she was invited to read a passage. It was a large Bible, very beautiful and surrounded with a celestial light. When Sister Agnes could recognize the references (Genesis 3:15), the voice of the angel was heard explaining in sort of a preamble that the passage had relationship with the tears of Mary, then continued:

"There is a meaning to the figure one hundred and one. This signifies that sin came into the world by a woman and it is also by a woman that salvation came to the world. The zero between the two signifies the Eternal God who is from all eternity until eternity. The first one represents Eve and the last the Virgin Mary." * Then the sister was again invited to reread the verse, and the angel left. At the same time the vision of the Bible disappeared.

After adoration Sister Agnes came at once to my office. She recounted the apparition and asked me to read verse 15 of chapter 3 of Genesis. She asked me to verify the passage before she herself would open a Bible. So I took out the modern Japanese translation by Father Barbaro

---

*For further explanation see *The Meaning of Akita.*

and found the following passage: *"I will place enmities between thee and the woman, between thy seed and hers. She will crush thy head and thou shalt lie in wait for her heel."*

Then she repeated to me the explanation of the angel concerning the meaning of the number 101... of the one hundred and one times that Our Lady's statue wept miraculously. At the moment I was not especially surprised. However, as the days passed I realized with growing emotion that the tears would flow no more and that the profound meaning had been elucidated by a passage from Scripture.

In verse 15 of the chapter in question, the sovereign God, the Absolute Being, makes the prophetic announcement to satan of the combat which will oppose him to the Virgin Mary throughout the ages. It is evident that the Seed of the Woman means Jesus comes into the world through Her and all those who will believe in Him. The Mystical Body of Christ is the community of believers of all generations of whom He is the Head. It is in union with the Church, the Mystical Body of Christ, that the Virgin has received from the Eternal Father the mission of fighting against satan and his cohorts until the end of the world.

This passage of Genesis is called protoevangelic and is considered as the first promise of a Savior made by God to man. It is also the first verse of the Bible making allusion to the Immaculate Conception of Mary, preserved from original sin and thus never under the domination of satan.

The apparitions of Our Lady of Lourdes have been considered as a commemoration of Her Immaculate Conception, the dogma of which had just been promulgated by Pope Pius IX, four years before the apparition.

The apparitions of Fatima might also be considered as a commemoration of Her Assumption. Pope Pius XII proclaimed the dogma of the Assumption on the first of November of the Holy Year of 1950, when one knows that the Holy Father at that time had the privilege of seeing again the Fatima "Miracle of the Sun" over the Vatican in that year.

The miraculous lachrymations of the statue of Our Lady in Akita had been explained by the angel with the aid of Scripture. The passage of Genesis suggests the war which opposes Mary and satan until the end of the world. Mary does not lead this combat alone. She is associated to the Mystical Body of Christ in union with all believers. As in the case of all of the apparitions of Our Lady, the call is one of reparation for sin and of a return to God.

The Complete Cure

The angel had said that, *"People ask a miracle greater than the tears; there will be no more."* And soon afterwards the statue wept for the last time. But of course we knew that there was to be another miracle, one which had been announced over and over and which would certainly be big enough to satisfy the commission: Sister Agnes, whose deafness had been declared incurable, was going to be absolutely and finally cured.

On the Feast of the Annunciation, a most important Feast for the Handmaids, Sister Agnes came to see me after the adoration and to say that the angel had appeared again. In substance this is what was said:

"Your deafness causes you to suffer doesn't it? The moment of the promised cure approaches. By the intercession of the Holy and Immaculate Virgin, exactly as the last time, before Him who is truly present in the Eucharist, your ears will be definitely cured in order that the work of the Most High may be accomplished. There will still be many sufferings and obstacles coming from outside. You have nothing to fear. In bearing them and offering them, you will be protected. Offer up and pray well. Transmit what I have told you to him who directs you and ask him for counsel and prayer."

As for me, I never doubted that the complete healing would come one day because the angel had said shortly before the first cure that it would be provisional, because God still wished this offering for sometime... I nevertheless was very impressed by the announcement of this prediction. It was impossible to foretell the date of the healing with so little detail. Nevertheless I told sister not to speak of it to anyone and to continue her normal activities.

Soon it was the month of May, the month consecrated to Mary. More than a month had passed since the announcement of the angel. On the Feast of Saint Joseph the Worker, the first of May, Sister Agnes received a message from the angel during adoration:

"Your ears will be definitely cured during this month consecrated to the Immaculate Heart of Mary. They will be cured as the last time by Him who is really present in the Eucharist. Those who will believe in this sign will receive many graces. There will be those who oppose, but you have nothing to fear."

If the cure was going to take place during the month of Mary, I told myself that it would certainly be a Sunday. And if it was going to happen again during the Benediction of the Blessed Sacrament, it would surely be during the ceremony of Benediction which happens on Sunday. The month of May had five Sundays. The first of May being a Saturday, the next day was the first Sunday of the month. That seemed nevertheless too soon. Certainly nothing permitted me to guess that it would be one Sunday rather than another. When I think back on it now, the last Sunday was Pentecost and furthermore the Vigil of the Feast of the Visitation, and seemed the most apt day for the realization of the promise made by the angel.

Whatever the case, one Sunday succeeded the other in the expectation of the prodigy and it was soon the Sunday of Pentecost. The hour of Benediction approached. That day there were fewer visitors than usual. The only persons from outside were Mr. and Mrs. Okuhara who had taken care of the scientific analysis of the liquids taken from the statue (truly there could not be more appropriate witnesses.)

After more than an hour of adoration I took the monstrance of the Blessed Sacrament, blessed the assemblage, then the bell sounded: *at that precise moment the ears of Sister Agnes opened* as the preceding time. When we had finished the divine praises, I heard her speak to me as before, "I have just received the grace of healing. I ask that one recite the Magnificat in thanksgiving." Restraining my emotion with difficulty ("It was therefore true!") I replaced the Host in the tabernacle and turning towards the assemblage I revealed publicly for the first time the content of the two predictions made by the angel sometime before, and announced to all that they had been realized at that moment. The hymn was sung with unusual force, sobs mixing with the voices, so great was the feeling of thanksgiving which overflowed from the heart of each.

The following morning, Sister Agnes presented herself to the eye and ear service of the Red Cross Hospital with which she was now acquainted for a long time. A detailed examination of the state of her ears showed that they had been totally cured. The doctor who seemed very impressed rose with a solemn air, and the nurses did the same, and bowed before her as he presented, "All my felicitations." Some days later Bishop Ito went in person to ask for a certificate of "miraculous cure." And despite the fact that doctors of this and another hospital had declared Sister Agnes incurable before, the certificate was refused, because apparently it is not permitted to inscribe the term "miraculous" in a medical certificate in these days.

Once again I would like the reader to consider the silence into which Sister Agnes was suddenly plunged from the beginning of the 16th of March, 1973, cut off from all exterior sound and which was a purification and an interior preparation for the messages she was to receive from Our Lady.

In the beginning of the Gospel of Saint Luke, the angel predicts to the priest of the Temple, Zachary, the coming birth of a child. To authenticate the promise, he predicts to him that he will be deaf and dumb until the accomplishment of that which appeared impossible.

Guided by her angel, Sister Agnes bore the trial of deafness well and received the unexpected grace of hearing words pronounced by Our Mother of Heaven. (This shows in passing that infirmity of the ears is no hindrance to receiving voices from the other World.)

The infirmity of the old Zachary was cured at the birth of John the Baptist and his mouth poured forth in torrents of praise for the Lord. The humiliation of the trial gave way to an immense thanksgiving for the gift received, giving way to unmixed joy.

The total deafness of Sister Agnes considered by all as a great cross, because it had been declared incurable, was cured in conformity to the prediction of the angel. And it is important to note that this complete cure took place after Bishop Ito had sent to the Holy See in Rome a dossier concerning all the events which had taken place up to this time.

Today the hearing of Sister Agnes is completely normal and one can even say that sometimes she has a "finer" ear than her companions.

The more one meditates on all these events which transformed the life of the convent of Yuzawadai, the working of Divine Providence appears ever more evident. One cannot fail to glorify the Lord for such great blessings.

Sister Agnes Sasagawa

Chapter Sixteen

Conclusion

The mysterious facts which I have described in the course of these 15 chapters came to an end on the 30th of May, 1982, Feast of Pentecost, with the complete curing of the ears of Sister Agnes. But it is fitting to take a last look back to a short time before the healing.

On that first of May of 1982, the angel appeared to Sister Agnes during her adoration before the Blessed Sacrament and told her that her ears would definitely hear during that month consecrated to Mary. And this was the last apparition of the guardian angel of Sister Agnes.

The theologian of the first commission of inquiry had told the Sister that she was recounting these words of the angel to herself and that the angel was an hallucination caused by a doubling of her personality. And she had not forgotten this warning which preoccupied her and she profited by the admonition of the angel on that day to ask:

"Are you the fruit of my personal imagination?"

"Not at all. I have shown myself to you up to this day to guide you, but I will not appear anymore." After having pronounced these words, the angel left her, disappearing into a cohort of angels who gave off a celestial light, the beauty of which could not be expressed in words.

When she told me this, I asked Sister Agnes to write down what she had seen, but she avowed that she was incapable of describing such a vision in words. But she had felt at that moment a profound consolation which had swept away at once all the doubts that she might have had on the nature of the "person" who was appearing to her.

Indeed the guardian angel has not appeared again. Even when the angel indicated to her a passage of the Bible while holding it open before her eyes, she only heard the angel's voice. When one considers that the signs relative to the statue ended and that the meaning of the message had been communicated, it is normal that the angel should no longer intervene in any special way from that time. It seems to me that another manifest sign of Divine Providence was the completion in December of 1982 of the reception center for the lay members of the community... as though everything followed a Divinely set timetable.

The story goes back to the 27th of February of the previous year. Through a master carpenter whom I knew, I went to see an abandoned farm on the site of which a new house was to be built four kilometers from our monastery.

I had previously admired the traditional architecture of old barns I had seen in Japan and with the need of increasing our space for receiving pilgrims, I had asked the carpenter to inform me if such a building should become available. The morning when I went to see it with three sisters of the community, after the morning Mass, I felt within myself that this building ought to be used for the reception of the lay members. In the car, bumping on the snowy roads, I spoke of this to my companions asking them to consider the building we were going to see with this perspective.

It was a single level building of about 330 square meters. It was 102 years old with enormous and very solid beams and everything that I could see was in a perfect state. With the accord of the sisters I settled with the proprietor who sold it to us without difficulty. If this occasion had arisen a year later, when I was ill, the realization of such a project would have been very much compromised.

Indeed I was suddenly stricken with loss of speech in February, 1983; the doctor had declared it incurable and said I would be incapable of ever taking up normal activity. But a year later, I improved enough to resume Holy Mass and little by little the homilies.

Thanks to this converted barn we can now receive not only the lay members of the community, but also many of the pilgrims who arrive in ever greater numbers since the event of Akita has been recognized officially as supernatural. After the Ordinary of the Diocese of Niigata officially authorized the veneration of the statue of Mary at Yuzawadai, the majority of the laity favorably welcomed the news but there still seemed to be some reticence on the part of some of the Catholic clergy. Some said that one should not go to Akita despite the recognition of the local

Bishop because Rome had not yet spoken. Rather than argue in my personal name, I will cite the recent work of Father Tatsuya Shimura entitled *"The Revelations of the Virgin at Fatima."* In the chapter *Recognition by the Church,* the author indicates that apparitions at Fatima were recognized by the Bishop of the diocese 13 years after, on the anniversary day of the apparitions. The following year, the Cardinal of Lisbon was in pilgrimage to the Cova of Fatima with a group of bishops in the presence of tens of thousands of people. Later Pope Paul VI, and then Pope John Paul II, personally went to Fatima.

But Fatima has never been "approved by Rome," nor has any other similar apparition. This is *always* left to the local bishop who, in matters of such importance, would rarely act without first consulting the Holy See.

In the fifth edition of his booklet entitled *The Virgin Mary Weeps in Japan,* the same author (Father Shimura) writes: "The revelations of the Virgin at Akita are exactly the same as those of Fatima, the seriousness of which is admitted by all. They are an urgent warning to mankind in danger of destruction and must not be taken lightly.

"Some think they should warn against it under the pretext that Rome has not yet made known its official position. But they seem to ignore that the Holy See delegates to the local bishop the authority of rejecting or recognizing such events and when there is such recognition, the Holy See approves only tacitly the declaration of the bishop."*

News of the recognition spread through all the dioceses of Japan and little by little, began to be known throughout the world. Pilgrims came in ever greater numbers to kneel before the statue with filial piety, to pledge before Her their act of consecration and to promise to respond to Her urgent requests.

From all that I have experienced, I have no doubt that the grace of Akita will spread to the ends of the earth for all the

*In June of 1988, Bishop Ito returned to Rome a third time, four years after he had issued the pastoral letter proclaiming the events of Akita to be supernatural. His Excellency was reassured by the Sacred Congregation of the Doctrine of the Faith that he had acted properly.

children of Mary. I seem already to see the glory of Our Lady shining on the entire world after the final victory of Her Immaculate Heart. To close, may I be permitted to borrow the words of Gamaliel in the Acts of the Apostles:

"Have nothing to do with these men, let them be. If this is man's design or man's undertaking, it will be overthrown; if it is God's, you will have no power to overthrow it. You would not willingly be found fighting against God." Acts Ch 5, 38-39.

Documents

Healing of a Brain Tumor in South Korea

Madam Theresa Chun, 46 years of age and mother of four children, was hospitalized from the spring of 1981 for a cerebral tumor. Treatment was of no avail and she fell into a coma. Some believers who had made a pilgrimage to Akita gave the photo of the Virgin to the family, counseling them to ask Her aid. The oldest sister and godmother of the sick person placed a picture of Our Lady of Akita on her pillow inviting friends and nurses also to pray (it was a Catholic clinic.) At sunrise on the 4th of August she regained consciousness in an inexplicable manner.

On the 15th of October 1983, some Korean pilgrims came to Akita with Father Oh Ki Saun; among them was Madam Chun and her eldest sister. They explained her cure which had been declared miraculous by Church authorities of Korea.

I interviewed her (with the assistance of Father Oh as translator): "What is your age?"

"46 years."

"When did you become sick?"

"The 3rd of July, 1981 (it is the sister who answers). She was examined the following day by Professor Kim Jang Je of the Catholic University of Gyonghwi in Seoul. She was found to have a brain cancer without hope of cure and told that it was useless to keep her longer in the hospital."

"When were you baptized a Catholic?"

"The 11th of April, 1981." Despite the difficulties of language, many questions and answers continued. The eldest sister, who had taken care of her, gave many details which can be summed up as follows:

At the time of this sickness Madame Chun had been baptized only a short time. She was completely ignorant of the events of Akita and also did not know about the photo of the weeping Virgin. It was her eldest sister and god-mother who had brought it to her. All were very sad and the eldest sister proposed some other treatments, including acupuncture, when suddenly the sick woman began to speak like a child and said, "I do not wish it. Jesus will cure me."

These words produced a strange impression on those present. It seemed as though she had fallen back into childhood. And hardly had she said these words than she lost consciousness and fell back into coma.

It is thanks to Father Oh that the sick person was brought into contact with the Virgin of Akita. This priest had come to Akita for the first time on the 26th of May, 1979. To his great astonishment he saw the tears flow. It lasted a short time, from ten minutes after four until ten minutes after six of the afternoon, but he was deeply touched and felt from that time the importance of his meeting with the Virgin of Akita. He carried back to Korea a great number of photos which he distributed to members of the Legion of Mary and fervent persons. Among them was the sister and godmother of Theresa whose life was held only by a thread. They placed their last hope in the solicitude of Mary who had manifested Herself in the sanctuary of Akita, so close to Korea. And what happened?

In the space of six months, Our Lady—as She was represented in the photograph—*appeared to the sick woman three times.* The first time was the 4th of August, 1981 at 3 o'clock in the morning while she was still in a coma. The Virgin wore a golden garment and held in Her arms a lamb as white as snow. She breathed three times on the forehead of Theresa who reported that the breath was alive, warm, and strong to such a point that she could see the fur of the lamb wave as Our Lady breathed on her. According to the testimony of those around, one heard the sick woman cry out from her coma, "Lamb! Lamb! Lamb!" but no one understood what that could mean.

The second apparition took place on the 15th of August, 1981 at 5 o'clock in the morning. Our Lady wore the same garment but no longer held the lamb. She first asked Theresa to recite the morning prayer with Her, and ordered her to rise. Then Theresa tried to get up, but did not at once succeed; she had to be helped by her sister who put her hand behind her back to hold her. She finally succeeded in standing up, but she still had to take the arm of her sister to walk.

The third apparition took place in the X-ray room of the hospital of Saint Paul. It was the 9th of December, 1981 while she was being examined to see whether or not she had been cured. This time Our Lady wore a garment of brilliant white altogether different from the preceding apparitions. Also she looked at Theresa with a smile before going back towards Heaven, always smiling.

The X-ray revealed a complete cure. After this miracle, the Church of Korea established a committee which met on March 3rd, 1983, in order to work towards the canonization of the 103 Korean martyrs. The authorities of the local church recognized that the miraculous cure of Madame Chun was due to the intercession of Our Lady of Akita and sent a letter to the Vatican signed by the bishops and members of the committee.

After the cure of Theresa, her sister showed her a photograph of Our Lady of Lourdes and one of Our Lady of Akita. Theresa did not hesitate to recognize the latter as the author of her cure.

We note that the Virgin Mary appeared three times for a single miracle. Each apparition carries a special meaning. The first time She appears to the sick woman while she is still in a coma. Even though she is in a state of unconsciousness, the vision is clearly perceptible. And it seemed that this apparition was impregnated in her spirit in an indelible fashion because she was able later to describe it in every detail. Such a living description cannot be given by someone unless they have lived the event.

In this first apparition the Virgin does not speak. She only breathes upon the forehead of Theresa and one is struck by the vigor of this breath which causes the fur of the lamb to wave. Could we not think that this breathing of theVirgin represents the Holy Spirit and that the lamb represents Jesus in the Eucharist? This would mean that the Virgin effected the miracle thanks to Jesus as Madame Chun had been inspired to hope. And even though Theresa did not yet come out of her comatose state, one could say that the sickness had already been cured.

The second apparition takes place on the day of the Assumption at 5 o'clock in the morning. The Virgin no longer carries the lamb, but comes only to awaken the one who has been already cured. She speaks to her for the first time, inviting her to recite with Her the morning prayer and to get up. Now that she is cured, she must pray and rise up. And she does it with the help of her sister. She must make known to everyone the cure that has taken place since the first apparition.

With the third apparition, in the X-ray room, one can say that Mary, author of the healing, wished to be present at the moment of the scientific recognition of the fact. The shining white garment, the smile of the Virgin as She mounts towards Heaven, adds to the sublimity of the scene. Surrounded by celestial glory, Mary comes to verify the complete healing, the victory obtained by the grace of the miracle.

Pastoral Letter of the Bishop of Niigata on the Subject of the Statue of the Virgin of Akita

John Shojiro Ito, Bishop of Niigata, 1984

I

To all members of the diocese, my blessing and my best wishes on this Feast of Easter. It is now twenty-two years that I have been bishop of the diocese of Niigata, named by His Holiness John XXIII in 1962. In conformity with the legislation of the Church I have reached the age of retreat and must give up my function. My thanksgiving goes to each one of you for prayer and cooperation which have permitted me, despite many difficulties, to fill my task up to the present day.

Before leaving you I must confide to you a preoccupation. It has to do with the series of mysterious events concerning a wooden statue of the Virgin Mary in the Institute of the Handmaids of the Eucharist. (The request for ecclesial recognition of this secular institute has been introduced in Rome.) This institute is found in Yuzawadai, Soegawa, Akita, in this diocese of Niigata (Japan). You are without doubt aware of these events through magazines, books, television, and so on.

When the first commission of inquiry was named in 1976, I publicly announced that it was necessary to abstain from all official pilgrimage and all particular veneration of this statue while the inquiry was underway. From that day I have made no declaration on this subject. Indeed, being a question of important events concerning the Church, one cannot treat them lightly. However, to keep silence at the time of leaving my function as bishop, since I have been at the heart of the events, would be a negligence with regard to my episcopal duties. For that reason I have decided to make a new declaration in the form of this pastoral letter.

Since 1973, when the events began, eleven years have passed. As that was the first time I was a witness of the rather extraordinary events, I went to Rome to the Sacred Congregation for the Doctrine of the Faith in 1975 where I consulted Monsignor Hamer, secretary of this Congregation and whom I already knew. He explained to me that such a matter belonged above all to the authority of the bishop of the place.

In 1976, I asked the archbishop of Tokyo for the creation of a commission of inquiry. This commission declared that it was not in a position to prove the supernatural events of Akita. In 1979, I presented to the Congregation a request for the formation of a second commission of inquiry which permitted us to examine the facts still more in detail.

In 1979, a letter of the Congregation, unfavorable to the events, came to the nunciature in Tokyo. But this letter contained some misunderstandings. Esteeming it my duty to restore the exactitude of the facts, I re-examined it all in 1982 at the time that the events came to an end. Through the intermediary of the Apostolic Nuncio in Tokyo, I sent the complete dossier, augmented with the new facts, to Rome.

At the time of my trip to Rome in the month of October last year (1983) I was able to meet with three personalities charged with the matter in the Congregation for the Doctrine of the Faith. At the end of this meeting we had decided that the dossier should again be submitted to prolonged examination.

II

The series of events relative to the statue of the Virgin Mary include the flowing of blood from the right hand of the statue, also a *perspiration* spreading a sweet perfume, perspiration so abundant that it was necessary to dry the statue. However, the most remarkable fact, in our opinion, and the most evident, is the overflowing of an aqueous liquid, similar to human tears, from the eyes of the statue of Our Holy Mother.

This began on the 4th of January, 1975 (Holy Year) and some *tears* flowed 101 times, until the 15th of September, 1981, Feast of Our Lady of the Seven Dolors. I was able myself to witness four lachrymations. About 500 persons have also been eyewitnesses. I twice tasted this liquid. It was salty and seemed to me truly human tears. The scientific examination of Professor Sagisaka, specialist in legal medicine in the faculty of medicine at the University of Akita, has proved that this liquid is indeed identical to human tears.

It is beyond human powers to produce water where there is none, and I believe that to do this the intervention of a nonhuman force is necessary. Moreover, it is not the question of pure water, but of a liquid secreted by a human body. It flowed only from the eyes of the statue, as tears flow, and that more than 100 times over a period of several years and before many numerous witnesses. It has been established that it could not have been by trickery or human maneuvers.

If these events are not natural one can envisage three causes. They would be due to:
1. Paranormal faculties of the human being;
2. Machinations of the devil;
3. A supernatural intervention.

I do not know well what could be paranormal faculties. However, certain individuals say that Agnes Katsuko Sasagawa, member of the Handmaids of the Servants of the Eucharist, and who was the one linked most especially to the events of Akita, might possess paranormal powers permitting her to transfer her own tears to the statue. For that however, it would be necessary, according to Professor Itaya of the Technical University of Tokyo (specialist in this field) that the interested person be aware of the fact in order to cause such paranormal powers to intervene. Now the tears have flowed from the statue when Agnes Sasagawa was sleeping and even when she was not aware of the event, being home with her family 400 kilometers from Akita. I think therefore that the hypothesis of such faculties can be put aside.

There are also persons who suppose that it is a question of a machination of the devil. If that is the case it ought to lead to evil effects for the faith. Not only have there not been such effects, but quite to the contrary there have been favorable effects. For example, a husband whose Catholic wife had for a long time recommended conversion decided to receive baptism after seeing the tears.

In another case, a former believer, separated from the Church for several decades, returned to the regular practice of our religion. And again, following a visit to the place, a believer resolved to work in evangelization. Alone she created two bases of evangelization and continues this work to the present day.

Furthermore, there are numerous reports of miraculous cures of sicknesses such as cancer, thanks to the mediation of the Virgin of Akita. I am going to mention two, the most proving.

One is the sudden cure of a Korean woman. Following cancer of the brain, she was reduced to a vegetable state from July, 1981. The Virgin of Akita appeared to her and told her to get up. Almost at once she was able to get up, having entirely recovered her health. This healing took place while priests and Korean women prayed to the Virgin of Akita for her cure and asked for a miracle in view of the canonization of the Korean martyrs. There are X-rays of this person taken during the sickness and after the complete cure. Even nonprofessionals can verify the cure. The authenticity of the X-rays is attested to by Dr. M. D. Tong-Woo-Kim, of the Hospital of Saint Paul in Seoul who took these X-rays, and also by Father Theisen, STD, president of the ecclesiastical tribunal of the archdiocese of Seoul.

All of the records have been sent to Rome. I went myself to Seoul (Korea) last year and was able to interview the person involved; I could thus assure myself of the truth of the facts of her miraculous cure. For her part the person came to Akita to thank Our Holy Mother.

The second case is the complete cure of the total deafness from which Agnes Sasagawa suffered. I will speak in detail of this later.

By such facts propitious to the faith and to physical health, it would seem to exclude that the events of Akita could be of diabolical origin. There remains therefore only the possibility of a supernatural intervention. It is in any event difficult to hold that it might be not a question of supernatural phenomena.

III

But why have such phenomena taken place? I ask if they are not with regard to the messages coming from the statue of the Virgin and perceived by the deaf ears of Agnes Sasagawa.

The first message was given to her on the morning of July 6th, 1973, first Friday of the month. A voice coming from the statue of Mary, always splendid, saying:

"My daughter, my novice, you have obeyed Me well in abandoning all to follow Me. Is the infirmity of your ears painful? Your deafness will be healed, be sure. Be patient. It is the last trial. Does the wound of your hand cause you to suffer? Pray in reparation for the sins of men. Each person in this community is my irreplaceable daughter. Do you say well the prayer of the Handmaids of the Eucharist? Then, let us pray it together:

"Most Sacred Heart of Jesus, truly present in the Holy Eucharist, I consecrate my body and soul to be entirely one with Your Heart being sacrificed at every instant on all the

altars of the world and giving praise to the Father, pleading for the coming of His Kingdom.

"Please receive this humble offering of myself. Use me as You will for the glory of the Father and the salvation of souls.

"Most Holy Mother of God, never let me be separated from your Divine Son. Please defend and protect me as Your special child. Amen.

"Pray very much for the Pope, the bishops and the priests."

Agnes Sasagawa lost her hearing when she was working as a catechist in the church of Myoko-kogen. Because of this deafness she was for a time in the hospital of Rosai in the city of Joetsu. Dr. Sawada diagnosed her total deafness as incurable and issued the documents permitting, for this reason, state subsidy. No longer being able to work as a catechist, she came to the Institute of the Handmaids of the Eucharist at Akita, where she began to live a life of prayer.

The second message, like the first time, was given by the voice coming from the statue of the Holy Virgin:

"My daughter, my novice, do you love the Lord? If you love the Lord, listen to what I have to say to you.

"It is very important. You will convey it to your superior.

"Many men in this world afflict the Lord. I desire souls to console Him to soften the anger of the Heavenly Father. I wish, with my Son, for souls who will repair by their suffering and their poverty for the sinners and ingrates.

"In order that the world might know His anger, the Heavenly Father is preparing to inflict a great chastisement on all mankind. With my Son, I have intervened so many times to appease the wrath of the Father. I have prevented the coming of calamities by offering Him the sufferings of the Son on the Cross, His Precious Blood, and beloved souls who console Him and form a cohort of victim souls. Prayer, penance and courageous sacrifices can soften the Father's anger. I desire this also from your community, that it love poverty, that it sanctify itself and pray in reparation for the ingratitude and outrages of so many men. Recite the prayer of the Handmaids of the Eucharist with awareness of its meaning; put it into practice; offer (whatever God may send) in reparation for sins. Let each one endeavor, according to capacity and position, to offer herself entirely to the Lord.

"Even in a secular institute prayer is necessary. Already souls who wish to pray are on the way to being gathered. Without attaching too much attention to the form, be faithful and fervent in prayer to console the Master."

The third and last message was given also by the voice coming from the statue of the Holy Virgin on the 13th of October in the same year:

"My dear daughter, listen well to what I have to say to you. You will inform your superior.

"As I told you, if men do not repent and better themselves, the Father will inflict a terrible punishment on all humanity. It will be a punishment greater than the deluge, such as one will never have seen before. Fire will fall from the sky and will wipe out a great part of humanity, the good as well as the bad, sparing neither priests nor faithful. The survivors will find themselves so desolate that they will envy the dead. The only arms which will remain for you will be the Rosary and the Sign left by my Son. Each day recite the prayers of the Rosary. With the Rosary, pray for the Pope, the bishops and the priests.

"The work of the devil will infiltrate even into the Church in such a way that one will see cardinals opposing cardinals, bishops against other bishops. The priests who venerate me will be scorned and opposed by their confreres, churches and altars sacked, the Church will be full of those who accept compromises and the demon will press many priests and consecrated souls to leave the service of the Lord.

"The demon will be especially implacable against souls consecrated to God. The thought of the loss of so many souls is the cause of my sadness. If sins increase in number and gravity, there will be no longer pardon for them."

This message is based on the condition if men do not repent and better themselves... I think that it is a serious warning, although one feels here the maternal love of Our Heavenly Mother in the words: "The sight of the loss of numerous souls makes me sad." If the promise contained in the first message of 1973 was not realized (Is your deafness painful to bear? You will soon be healed) one would be able to doubt the veracity of these messages. But this promise was kept nine years after the beginning of the sickness.

Before this happened, a person similar to an angel announced to Agnes Sasagawa (the 25th of March, and the 1st of May, 1982): *"Your deafness causes you to suffer doesn't it? The moment of the promised cure approaches. By the intercession of the Holy and Immaculate Virgin, exactly as the last time, before Him Who is truly present in the Eucharist, your ears will be definitely cured in order that the work of the Most High may be accomplished. There will still be many sufferings and obstacles coming from outside. You have nothing to fear."*

Effectively on the last Sunday of the month of Mary, the 30th of May, 1982, Feast of Pentecost, at the moment of Benediction of the Blessed Sacrament her ears were cured completely and instantly.

That same evening she telephoned to me and we conversed normally. On the following 14th of June, I visited Doctor Arai of the Eye and Ear Division of the Hospital of the Red Cross of Akita who had verified the complete deafness of Agnes Sasagawa at the moment she arrived in Akita nine years before.

I asked his impression. He was amazed at this complete cure. Doctor Sawada of the Rosai de Joetsu who had been the first to examine her when she became deaf, has now issued a medical certificate dated June 3rd, 1982, attesting that following minute examinations of the auditive capacities, he certifies that there is no further anomaly in the two ears of Agnes Sasagawa.

I have known Agnes Sasagawa for ten years. She is a woman sound in spirit, frank and without problems; she has always impressed me as a balanced person. Consequently the messages she says that she has received did not appear to me to be in any way the result of imagination or hallucination.

As for the content of the messages received, there is nothing contrary to Catholic doctrine or good morals, and when one thinks of the actual state of the world, the warning seems to correspond to it in many points.

Having set down here my experiences and my reflections with regard to the events relative to the statue of the Holy Virgin of Akita, I esteem it my duty, as Ordinary of the place, to respond to the requests of the faithful to give pastoral directives on this subject. It is only the bishop of the diocese in question who has the power of recognizing a fact of this kind. The Congregation of the Doctrine of the Faith has given me directives in this regard.

I have been in constant relation with the Institute of the Handmaids of the Eucharist since its creation, and thus I know exactly the situation of this Institute and of its members. In studying the history of the apparitions of the Virgin Mary up to this day, I am aware that it is always the bishops of the place who have authorized the veneration of the Virgin Mary when she has manifested Herself in their diocese.

After long prayer and mature reflection, I draw the following conclusions in my position as Bishop of Niigata:

1. After the inquiries conducted up to the present day, one cannot deny the supernatural character of a series of inexplicable events relative to the statue of the Virgin which is found in the convent of the Institute of the Handmaids of the Eucharist at Yuzawadai, Soegawa, Akita (diocese of Niigata.)

Nor does one find in it elements contrary to Catholic faith and good morals.

2. Consequently, I authorize throughout the entire diocese, with which I am charged, the veneration of the Holy Mother of Akita, while awaiting that the Holy See publishes definitive judgment on this matter.

And I ask that it be remembered that even if the Holy See later publishes a favorable judgment with regard to the events of Akita, it is a question only of a private revelation which is not a point of doctrine. Christians are bound to believe only content of Divine revelation (closed after the death of the last Apostle) which contains all that is necessary for salvation.

Nevertheless, the Church, until now, has equally taken into consideration private revelations insofar as they fortify the faith. For reference, I cite the following texts of the document on Catholic Doctrine:

"The saints and the angels having been conformed to the Will of God, receive from Him grace and glory in abundance and it is just to venerate them because this results in offering praise and thanksgiving to God Himself. Among the saints the Virgin Mary receives a special veneration. Indeed, She is not only the Mother of Our Savior who is God, but also the Mother of us all, and it is as Mother that She intercedes for us, full of Divine grace more than all the saints and angels." (Article 72)

"One venerates the statues and images of Christ and of the saints to sustain the faith, to adore Christ, to venerate the saints. This act thus becomes praise to God." (Article 170)

Finally, I beg God that He accord to you all abundant graces, with my Apostolic Benediction.

Niigata, Feast of Easter, April 22, 1984

Signed, John Shojiro Ito, Bishop

Above: Bishop Ito explains the message of Akita to a group of U.S. pilgrims in the Akita chapel. His Excellency said: "It is the message of Fatima."

Above: Blue Army Akita pilgrimage from the U.S. with Father Tatsuya Shimura and Japanese Blue Army members outside Tokyo Cathedral. Father Shimura wrote the first book on the Akita events.

Below: Convent of the apparitions.

201.

Lachrymations:	Date:	Time:	# of Witnesses:
1	01/04/75	09:30 a.m.	20
2	"	12:30 p.m.	20
3	"	06:45 p.m.	18
4	03/06/75	12:45 p.m.	15
5	05/01/76	07:30 a.m.	20
6	"	09:20 a.m.	--
7	"	05:00 p.m.	--
8	"	09:40 p.m.	30
9	05/02/76	12:30 p.m.	55
10	05/13/76	12:50 p.m.	35
11	07/26/78	09:00 p.m.	46
12	08/31/78	02:45 p.m.	18
13	09/15/78	05:00 p.m.	16
14	10/11/78	08:15 a.m.	23
15	10/21/78	07:30 a.m.	20
16	11/04/78	07:30 p.m.	13
17	11/06/78	07:35 p.m.	18
18	11/09/78	08:10 a.m.	13
19	11/13/78	08:10 a.m.	12
20	12/05/78	04:20 p.m.	16
21	12/07/78	08:40 p.m.	18
22	12/25/78	02:15 p.m.	60
23	01/24/79	07:00 p.m.	13
24	03/04/79	05:40 p.m.	13
25	03/07/79	01:45 p.m.	10
26	03/25/79	09:20 p.m.	13
27	03/27/79	05:25 p.m.	11
28	03/31/79	05:10 p.m.	23
29	04/04/79	09:20 a.m.	20
30	04/08/79	09:30 a.m.	23
31	04/09/79	02:45 p.m.	16
32	05/01/79	04:00 p.m.	19
33	05/05/79	06:45 p.m.	20
34	05/06/79	04:10 p.m.	--
35	05/09/79	04:30 p.m.	14
36	05/10/79	12:30 p.m.	17
37	05/13/79	08:00 a.m.	--
38	"	12:05 p.m.	23
39	05/19/79	11:50 a.m.	15
40	05/20/79	09;30 a.m.	--
41	05/21/79	06:20 p.m.	13
42	05/22/79	02:10 p.m.	11
43	05/26/79	04:35 p.m.	11
44	05/27/79	09:20 a.m.	12
45	05/29/79	11:55 a.m.	15
46	"	08:20 p.m.	11
47	05/31/79	10:30 a.m.	13
48	06/02/79	09:00 a.m.	12
49	06/03/79	10:05 a.m.	40

50	06/05/79	08:10 p.m.	13
51	06/06/79	07:30 a.m.	13
52	06/07/79	03:30 p.m.	19
53	06/09/79	08:00 a.m.	10
54	06/10/79	09:20 a.m.	12
55	06/12/79	11:15 a.m.	10
56	"	07:40 p.m.	18
57	06/14/79	12:50 p.m.	12
58	06/15/79	05:30 p.m.	10
59	06/16/79	05:40 p.m.	13
60	06/17/79	11:00 a.m.	25
61	06/21/79	04:32 p.m.	18
62	06/22/79	05:23 p.m.	17
63	06/23/79	03:30 p.m.	40
64	06/25/79	05:25 p.m.	15
65	06/26/79	12:50 p.m.	13
66	06/28/79	02:20 p.m.	15
67	06/29/79	11:30 a.m.	06
68	07/01/79	11:10 a.m.	13
69	07/06/79	07:20 a.m.	14
70	07/07/79	12:15 a.m.	11
71	07/08/79	09:15 a.m.	14
72	"	06:15 p.m.	15
73	07/10/79	05:20 p.m.	12
74	07/11/79	07:20 a.m.	12
75	"	07:20 p.m.	15
76	07/13/79	09:40 a.m.	10
77	"	02:00 p.m.	22
78	07/14/79	09:00 a.m.	24
79	07/16/79	11:00 a.m.	12
80	07/18/79	11:00 a.m.	13
81	07/02/79	04:30 p.m.	14
82	07/22/79	12:35 p.m.	10
83	"	07:25 p.m.	17
84	07/23/79	05:15 p.m.	18
85	07/24/79	05:20 p.m.	14
86	"	07:10 p.m.	14
87	07/25/79	08:15 a.m.	30
88	"	12:30 p.m.	24
89	07/26/79	08:45 a.m.	50
90	07/27/79	05:25 p.m.	46
91	07/28/79	03:20 p.m.	46
92	07/29/79	01:20 p.m.	17
93	07/30/79	03:05 p.m.	20
94	07/31/79	03:00 p.m.	16
95	"	04:45 p.m.	16
96	12/08/79	00:10 a.m.	20
97	"	11:28 p.m.	26
98	01/06/81	08:50 a.m.	18
99	08/22/81	01:00 p.m.	44
100	09/12/81	08:44 a.m.	13
101	09/15/81	02:00 p.m.	65

ttt